Parents Guide
to
Top 10
Dangers
Teens Face

FOCUS ON THE FAMILY®

Parents Guide to Top 10 Dangers Teens Face

Stephen Arterburn & Jim Burns

TYNDALE

Tyndale House Publishers, Wheaton, Illinois

PARENTS GUIDE TO TOP 10 DANGERS TEENS FACE

Library of Congress Cataloging-in-Publication Data

Arterburn, Stephen, 1953–
    Parents guide to top 10 dangers teens face / Stephen
Arterburn and Jim Burns.
            p.   cm.
    Includes bibliographical references.
    ISBN 1-56179-689-1
    1. Parenting—Handbooks, manuals, etc.   I. Burns, Jim,
1953– . II. Title.
HQ755.8.A735   1995
649'.1—dc20   95-30774
                                               CIP

A Focus on the Family book
Published by Tyndale House Publishers, Wheaton, Illinois.

This book was previously published under the title
Steering Them Straight.

Editors: Stephen and Amanda Sorenson
Designer: AvreaFoster
Cover photo: Tony Stone Images

    00 01 02 03 / 9 8 7 6 5 4

To the thousands of parents who have inspired us by their determination to persevere through the tough times and rejoice when they see the results of their dedication.

To our two favorite sets of parents:

Robert and Donna Burns

and

Walter and Clara Arterburn

Contents

Acknowledgments

Preface

1. The Death of Innocence 1

2. The Evolution of the Dysfunctional Family . 13

3. The Transitional Generation 49

4. Growing Up at Risk 67

5. Sex 83

6. Substance Abuse 99

7. Sexual Abuse 131

8. Suicide 143

9. Satanism 157

10. Homosexuality 171

11. AIDS 197

12. Pornography 213

13. Runaways 233

14. Eating Disorders 255

15. Five Positive Parenting Principles
    to Prevent Crisis 273

16. Influencing Young People's
   Spiritual Values 297

17. Hope for Parents Who Think
   They've Failed 311

   30 Ways to Keep Communication Open
   with Your Child 317

   Endnotes 321

   Referrals 329

   Books and Resources 333

Acknowledgments

A special thanks to Peter and Gail Ochs of Fieldstone and Frank Trane for helping make the "Kids in Crisis" seminars possible. Those seminars are the foundation of this material.

Erin Graffy did a tremendous job on research and development. We appreciate her dedication to this project.

Gwen Ellis stepped on board at Focus on the Family and into the middle of our work. We are deeply grateful to her for allowing her talent to become part of this book.

Preface

As a parent, you have the ability to help mold your children into healthy, thriving people. Of course, there will be bumps and bruises along the way. There will be detours and even wrong turns. However, the good and bad news is that your children are made of clay. You can make a difference in shaping their lives. In this book, we hope you will discover that it's never too early or too late to start helping your children become all that God created them to be.

Our simple goal is to help you reduce the "risk factors" and keep your children and family out of crisis. We work every day with children and families in crisis, and we believe parents can learn from their own mistakes and victories and from those of others.

We've never met a family that works exactly like the ones portrayed in shows we grew up on, such as "The Cosby Show," "Father Knows Best," or our all-time favorite, "Leave It to Beaver." But we've met hundreds of families that are using the principles in this book and are thriving. Those families may go three steps forward and two steps back, but they are still moving in the right direction.

The parents in those families decide they will not repeat destructive patterns of the past. If they are determined to resolve their problems rather than reproducing them, they could be the transitional generation leading out of dysfunction and into a generation of healthy, responsible human beings. We invite you to join a new army of parents who are creating that brighter future. They are breaking the chains of their past and changing the course of their families.

Parents Guide to Top 10 Dangers Teens Face is our attempt to help you better understand what you can do beyond loving your children, especially during the tough times all parents face, and to provide the inspiration and tools needed to make a positive difference. When it comes to parenting, one principle underlies everything: Love is not always enough, but it is the beginning. We thank you for loving your children enough to read the words that follow.

Steve Arterburn
Laguna Beach, California

Jim Burns
Dana Point, California

CHAPTER ONE

The Death of Innocence

Because you have picked up this book and started reading, you probably are interested in kids and deeply love at least a few of them. You are probably more interested in what's going on in your home than in what's happening in American culture. Yet it's important for all parents to quickly review the cultural trends of our society and understand why our kids have become a generation in trouble.

Our journey begins with profound words by Carla Koehl:

> There are, unfortunately, no SATs to measure maturity: no tests to determine how a student handles frustration, resolves conflicting choices, or develops intellectual interests in people and events and ideas that are older

than yesterday. These are qualities of character that are best developed at home, and the absence of these values in the young, many experts believe, reflects a lack of parental concern. The irony is that we have the best group of educated parents in history doing the least for their own kids. . . .

Ultimately it's a question of cultural values. What young people see enshrined in the media and malls of America are, after all, the values adults put there: consumerism, narcissism, and the instant gratification of desire. When those change, so will American youth.[1]

Those are tough words that should not make us feel guilty but should, instead, motivate us to look at ourselves before we criticize the culture of our youth. Much of the change in the values of American youth has occurred because we adults have allowed our cultural values to slip away.

When June Cleaver said, "Ward, I'm worried about the Beaver," she wasn't referring to crack cocaine, pornography, or suicide. Her primary concern was probably that he not turn out to be as obnoxious as Eddie Haskell. Times have changed since those days of innocence were reflected on the screens of black-and-white television sets. The days when children ran barefoot and picked dandelions ended with the death of innocence, when children were forced to grow up before their childhood was completed. The crisis with kids hit when innocence was abandoned early for a harder world. Childhood today presents challenges that contemporary adults never faced as children. For many children, the recklessness of youth has been replaced by a desperate search for a means of survival.

The picture of America's kids and the struggles they face is not pretty. Within the next 30 minutes:

- 29 kids will attempt suicide.
- 57 adolescents will run away from home.
- 14 teenagers will give birth out of wedlock.
- 22 girls will get abortions.
- 686 kids will use one of many drugs.
- 188 will abuse alcohol.[2]

Those statistics often don't mean much until they happen to your child. Then, suddenly, they have great meaning. If you think about them, though, they do clarify the fact that the world of our children is much different from the one we knew. When we were teenagers, we had the feeling of innocence. But for many kids today, that feeling left long ago.

Let's look at the variety of sources that have killed the innocence of our young.

Mass Media

Thousands of images of immorality played out in movies, videos, MTV, and vulgar sitcoms have seared the consciences of our young. These reflections of a sordid reality, produced by mass media that run rampant over Judeo-Christian values, haven't gone unnoticed. Our children have grafted the filth they have seen into their hearts. One need only search the headlines of virtually any newspaper to see the documentation of a young generation that is acting out the horrors portrayed on wide screens across America.

In it's 1994 national survey on risky behavior among young people, the Centers for Disease Control and Prevention found that 40 percent of the teens polled had sexual intercourse by the ninth grade. Seventy-two percent of those surveyed had sex by their senior year in high school. One in five reported having four or more sexual partners.[3]

A 15-year-old New Yorker says that boys expect to sleep with a girl after a couple of dates. The girls often carry cab fare because the boys ditch them when they refuse to have sex. In more conservative Dallas, Texas, teens will wait a few months and then have sex anyway. One survey revealed that among boys, 86 percent were having sex by age 19, which is up from 78 percent in 1979.[4] The world has changed and, in the sexual arena, for kids, it is not better.

Graphic evidence of the deterioration of our young people's morals was presented in November 1989, on CBS's production of "48 Hours." In that show it was revealed that half of American adolescents are sexually active, which produces about a million pregnancies a year. At one Fairfax, Virginia, hospital, a baby is born to a teenager every 15 hours. One-third of the teen girls visiting a Nova Teen Health Center in Fairfax show abnormal pap smears, indicative of diseases that result from multiple sexual partners. At

Grady Hospital in Atlanta, 40 percent of births are to women in their teens. One or two a week are to 14- or 15-year-olds. And finally, the United States government supports teenage mothers through welfare payments to the tune of $20 billion a year. That's $200 per taxpayer.[5] And the saddest part of all is that this astronomical financial cost is nothing compared to the extreme emotional burden brought on by too much sex, too early. These emotional burdens were highlighted in a National Survey of Family Growth, which revealed that 9 percent of all girls under 18 become mothers and another 9 percent obtain abortions.[6]

Children are fed an almost constant diet of scenes depicting sexual acts through various media sources. Adults abuse children by the thousands, and in turn, those children may abuse the children of future generations. Victims all too easily become victimizers as the agony of reproduced sin continues.

The Occult

This old threat is gaining new popularity and saturating the lifestyles of adolescents. Authorities say America is witnessing an epidemic of concern over Satan and his minions, especially among adherents of fundamentalist Christianity. Ritual abuse is only part of it. This new rise in interest has been heightened by numerous reports of sexual ritual abuse conducted at the hands of Satan-worshipers. The interest is so keen that when NBC ran a documentary entitled "Exposing Satan's Underground," it was the highest rated documentary ever to air on NBC.[7]

The beginnings of Satan worship are subtle. It has been reported that Shawn Sellers, who sits on death row for the murder of his parents, became involved in satanism when he let an interest in the Dungeons & Dragons game become an obsession. He performed rituals while covered in blood that was sometimes mixed with wine and urine, and he began taking drugs.

Sergeant Emon, a police officer on a metropolitan police force, said in a *Los Angeles Times* article that youngsters become involved with Satan worship because of lack of direction. They spend their time looking for power, seeking gratification of their ego, and fulfilling all their lustful desires. They have forsaken the power found in the Creator and exchanged it for a chance to access the evil deceiver of the universe.

Crime

Crimes of violence involving our kids are at an all-time high. More than six million crimes are committed each year against young people who are between the ages of 12 and 19. Three hundred thousand children are attacked at school every month. For example, 15-year-old Michael Thomas left home for school wearing a new, $100 pair of AirJordan basketball shoes—the Mercedes-Benz of athletic footwear. The next day James David Martin, age 17, was wearing the new sneakers, and Thomas lay dead in a field near the school. James was later arrested for the murder.[8] This was the third killing at that school motivated by envy of another person's clothing. A police officer was quoted as saying, "This obsession with clothing is fueled by the visual media and advertising. It is nurtured by overindulgent parents and is reinforced by youthful peer pressure and the child's overriding desire to 'fit in.'"

Drugs

The drug crisis has also infiltrated the ranks of our youngest children. The liquor industry appeals to younger consumers with clever dogs and heroes who hawk the seductive syrup. Kids drink to get drunk and escape reality with the latest designer drugs. God has been abandoned for the latest thrills. Almost 40 percent of all sixth graders will consume alcohol, thanks to the advent and prolific advertising of wine coolers.[9] In Pennsylvania, a group of even younger children developed a make-believe drug ring and used sugar for cocaine and grass for marijuana. They even had a ledger to record each transaction. Upon seeing this, one official said, "We have lost the war on drugs."

It's no mystery that America has lost the drug war. Drug-prevention programs in America's schools are primarily based on the belief that parents should teach their children how to drink and take drugs responsibly (as if a 14-year-old could responsibly consume an illegal and addictive substance). These programs are void of traditional values and deny or ignore the concept that some behaviors are right and others are wrong.

School officials at Bainbridge High School in

Washington State admit that their drug-prevention program, which was designed to help kids use drugs and alcohol responsibly, has failed. In a Wall Street Journal interview, a kid from Bainbridge High School said, "Drugs are as plentiful as potato chips." [10] The saddest part of this story is that the drug program at Bainbridge High is the model for many other schools across our country. With 70 percent of the Bainbridge kids either drunk or doing drugs every week, we can only expect the problem to worsen if school systems don't turn back to traditional Judeo-Christian values.

Intellectualism Replacing Morality

People have turned to intellectualism as if they could become so smart that their intellect would override immorality. Rather than refine morality to a higher level, intellectualism has decimated it, placed it into a small box, and labeled it "old-fashioned religion." The problem of morality has never been one of intellect. The most intelligent among us may also be immoral. Morality is always a problem of the will. The submission of the will to high standards of morality far outweighs any increase in intelligence or acquisition of knowledge. In most cases, the brightest among us also believe they have little need for God.

Liberal Religion

Liberalism has drained our children of their potential. It has also drained from its teaching the supernatural power of the living God and the sacrificial

Christ, who was pure and innocent. The move away from traditional Christian teachings has left our children without a spiritual foundation. Our children, too, make up their own religious interpretations and create their own philosophies, leaving Christ far behind.

New Age Movement

This has filled a generation with false hopes and Shirley MacLainiacs who claim to leave their bodies as they evolve into gods sculpted into their own likeness. Like people seeking the stars of fame and fortune in a wax museum, New Age parents have found the perfect imitation of Christianity. Believing they have seen the real thing, they raise their children on the notions of a fake faith and a fake god.

Complacent Christians

Our children's innocence has also died because complacent church leaders would rather preach angrily against homosexuals, for example, than help parents guide their children to avoid homosexuality or help them deal with the reality that their children have chosen to live a homosexual lifestyle. Church leaders often rail against sinful behavior while neglecting to reach out to lost strugglers and welcome them back to God. Many ministers preach against drunkenness rather than offering opportunities to educate parents on how to raise kids without drugs. Complacent church leaders preach against abortion rather than raising money so teenagers can raise their children or building a home where kids can have their kids and adopt them out to loving parents. Within the church, some Christians rail against materialism rather than showing the wealthy, by example, how money can be used to help people with great needs.

We Can Make a Difference

To reverse this tide, a group of repentant and committed parents is needed who will come alongside kids and make a difference. Parents can help kids find a path back to the values of our Judeo-Christian heritage. That's what Christ would do for our kids. He'd meet them where they are. He'd help them change the face of the earth—one child at a time. The heart of America can be changed as we bring kids back from crisis—one family, one community, and one generation at a time.

Our society is like a boy operating a new electric train. For a short time, he is satisfied with watching the motor glide the wheels across the tracks. But the thrill is short-lived. Soon he has to break the rules, turning up the dial on the transformer. He lets the train rip faster and faster until it derails. The thrill is in the derailment—the destruction of it all—not in the natural order of things. The moral future of our country hangs in the balance. Now is the time to save the kids.

In order for the innocence in our children to be reborn, parents who want to make a difference must make a new commitment. When they are willing to sacrifice and pay the price, they will become a transitional generation—a generation of hope. As the world stands looking for answers, we parents can rejoice that in Christ we have the ultimate answer, and we must find new ways to communicate the hope of Christ to today's kids in crisis and to all the other kids who have not succumbed to society's pressure. The world's solutions produce more and more despair. We must accept the responsibility of carrying the reality of God to them. When we do, our children will have hope.

> Our children too shall serve him, for they shall hear from us about the wonders of the Lord; generations yet unborn shall hear of all the miracles he did for us. (Ps. 22:30-31, *The Living Bible*)

We can make a great difference today. Many industries would go out of business if American parents woke up and trained their children to discern right from wrong.

Fueled by profiteers and capitalism gone awry, the liquor industry talks of moderation but makes millions off those who consume alcohol by the gallon. If those who drank decided to have no more than one drink when they did drink, the beer and liquor industry would die.

Abstinence among teens would kill the condom companies, which shun a sweeping new morality for our country.

Pharmaceutical companies that dispense birth-control pills count on kids being in crisis.

The abortionist would never preach sexual abstinence.

Those who peddle pornography and X-rated movies have a vested interest in seeing that our children don't tune in to the Ten Commandments and the virtues therein.

But it's not too late to stop the destruction of our children. We can become the transitional generation that will save thousands of children from the destruction that comes when God is relegated to second place.

CHAPTER TWO

The Evolution of the Dysfunctional Family

If there was a buzzword for the eighties, it was *dysfunctional*. This word seemed to come out of nowhere and soon was used to describe everything that didn't work. That is perhaps the best way to describe what *dysfunctional* means. It simply describes something that doesn't work. When a family doesn't work—when a family is broken or hurting—it's dysfunctional.

Although the word *dysfunctional* is relatively new, family problems certainly are not. History is replete with families that were, quite frankly, a mess. The families described in the Bible are no exception. God didn't spare us the details of how dysfunctional some of His people were. As we'll see later, the very lineage of Christ is full of families that were dysfunctional to the point of rape, murder, and rebellion against parents.

One word that describes a dysfunctional family's experience is often neglected. That word is *pain*. Those who live and grow up in dysfunctional families hurt deeply. Often their pain is so strong that it thwarts their efforts to succeed. They may know how to succeed and want to do so; but because of their intense emotional pain, they are driven to merely find some way to hang on to life, to survive.

It's amazing what some family members will do to survive. We can hope that their chosen behaviors or patterns of survival allow them to exist long enough to discover their pain, resolve it, and grow beyond it. This book, for some, could be a first step in resolving painful past issues and moving out of a survival mode and into a successful way of living.

Our knowledge of dysfunctional families doesn't come from just a textbook. We're both from what could be considered classic examples of dysfunctional families. We don't say this to hurt our families. In fact, our parents are very good people who raised their children in the stoic mode that most parents have used during the past two or three decades. We let you in on that secret about our past so you'll know that we understand your pain. We have lived it and, like you, have survived.

Our families' problems were not blatant like those most often written about. In our homes, no one was sexually abused or had a parent who was intentionally neglectful. The problems were much more subtle. In homes where subtle problems exist, it's often more difficult to identify and try to correct the problems. For example, we want to tell you about the Tosca family, a family that didn't appear to be sick or troubled, a family that looked good on the outside. Inside, however, the pain of family dysfunction seeped into the soul of every family member.

Most people would never have known the problems in the Tosca family if their tragedy had not made the local newspaper headlines. The townspeople were shocked to pick up the morning paper and read, "Tosca Youth Found Hanging in Basement." It was a cold, hard message to a town that had been unaware of the pain and heartache that tormented one of its high school heroes. The note young John Tosca left behind thanked the townspeople for their love and direction and explained that the pressure was just too great. He committed suicide to escape pressure he couldn't tolerate. So, unlike most of us from dysfunctional families, he didn't survive. A deep look inside his family provides insights into why that happened.

Antony Tosca was hard-working, a self-starter and an engineer who liked his house and family of seven to run in a neat, organized fashion. He came from a Swiss household of six children that was just as perfectionistic. When it came to keeping things orderly, no one was better at it or demanded more from his family.

Antony was immensely proud of his accomplishments and his children. Being proud was part of his problem. The phrases "I'm sorry" and "I'm wrong" weren't in his vocabulary, nor was true humility a part of his nature. He was the ultimate walking facade. What other people saw on the outside had nothing to do with what was really going on inside. Not even Antony knew what was inside. That part of him that felt and cared had been sealed up long ago when he was still a child. He was the typical macho, stoic male, full of emotions and intense feelings but unable to identify or know how to express them appropriately.

Since he couldn't connect with his own emotions, Antony's connection to his wife and children was superficial. It lacked intimacy. Although he cared deeply for his five daughters and two sons and they knew it intellectually, he wasn't a warm person, so they found it difficult to feel his love in an emotional way. He was so "distant."

He wasn't cruel or mean, but even his infrequent compliments were tinged with "it-could-be-better" implications that came from his compulsive perfectionism. Being raised by Antony meant inheriting the feeling that nothing you could do was good enough for him, God, or anyone else.

Before John committed suicide, he spent many years trying to measure up. But he never could. Even a night of high school football heroics, when the town cheered as he ran or threw for touchdown after touchdown, wasn't good enough for his dad. Antony would be awake when his son returned home following the after-game celebration. Sitting in his recliner, having relived every minute of the game while John was celebrating, Antony would start by saying, "That was a pretty good game, but next time I know you can do better." Then he would point out what he thought were John's mistakes and errors in judgment. He didn't limit his criticism of John to the football field, either. While looking over John's homework, he would typically make a comment like, "That looks great, John. But you should have used a different tool. That would have made the edge straighter."

The other children were also victims of Antony's tyranny. "Why are you going to use that paint, Lars? Why would you choose that color for your cabinet? You should use white; it'll match better." Or he'd say, "Brigette may think she did a great job sewing the dining room draperies, but she left the scissors out and didn't put away the needles."

If the Tosca children felt adequate at anything, they acquired that feeling because someone outside the family had taken a special interest in them and offered unconditional praise for accomplishments. But no matter what someone outside the family did to assist them, none of the children ever felt good enough at the core of their being. Each one, especially John, had a nagging feeling of inferiority quite similar to the one Antony lived with and tried to deny through his extremely controlled world of order.

Antony seemed to have everything under control for himself. He seemed to do everything in moderation and never used drugs or alcohol. Yet he failed to notice his mood swings, which were almost parallel to an alcoholic's . . . but without the liquor. His emotional responses were irregular and unpredictable. He swung from gloomy pessimism, intense anger, and negative faultfinding to ambivalent and noncommittal distancing to expansive and unrealistic optimism.

Some of his mood swings may have reflected his personal issues or problems. But because Mr. Tosca was closed off emotionally and couldn't express intimacy, no one else in the family could know what prompted his feelings or begin to understand how to help him. Because he didn't know how to deal with emotions (the emotions he didn't think he had), his anger bubbled up from within. Still, he rarely raised his voice or even swore. He was proud to say, "I never get mad, I get even." But his anger brewed under the surface, simmered under the skin, and ate away at his stomach.

It should be no surprise that, like his father, John also never learned to express himself or reveal his pain to another person. He stewed in his anguish until it drove him over the edge. Just like his father, he didn't get angry; he got even. Nothing could have pained his parents more than seeing their model son hanging from a pipe by the belt they had given him for Christmas.

Long before John's death, Mrs. Tosca knew that her husband's behavior was unreasonable, but she regularly made excuses to the children for his moods. She would deny her own pleasures to accommodate his mental and emotional state. In fact, denial was part of her coping mechanism—the way she handled his unpredictable behavior. She was a classic codependent, determined to keep the problem contained while it grew larger and more destructive every day.

"You have to realize that your papa is under tremendous stress at work," Anamarie Tosca would tell the children. "You've got to understand that when you don't have your rooms clean, it makes him angry." There were always excuses for his behavior, but never any accountability. Her naive excuses only drove the children more and more into believing that if only they were "better," the world would be different and their family could be what it was meant to be. This tyranny of self-imposed guilt would have been too much for most of us to handle unless we, too, learned to survive in the emotional isolation and despair that the Toscas had. The pressure was too much for John.

Anamarie had no idea that covering up for her husband would lead to the death of her son. She never dreamed that her actions were just as destructive as her husband's unreasonable behavior. She prided herself on being the "sensible one." *After all, she reasoned, my husband has all the problems. I'm the martyr. I have to put up with this unreasonable man.* The martyr role was, in a superficial way, good for her self-esteem, because as the children grew, she knew she had their sympathy and understanding in dealing with her husband. But Anamarie would be surprised to learn that she didn't have her children's respect. They saw that she lacked the self-esteem to stand up to her husband. Long ago, they had looked to her to fix or change the family. They believed she had the power to do it. They had also watched her become a victim of the same trap that ensnared them. As their hope for change faded, so did their respect for her. Perhaps John's decision to choose death came out of a sense that not even Mom could help.

Although Anamarie considered herself the antithesis of her husband, in many ways both of them were quite similar. Mrs. Tosca avoided intimacy. She had no close friends with whom she could share deep feelings. Her pride didn't allow her to seek counseling. She used the same excuse thousands have used: "What would people think?" So she couldn't discover her deep fear of abandonment. Instead, she projected her fear to her children through negativity. "Don't do that," she'd say. "What if you fail?" Or, "Be careful of those kinds of people. . . ." Her statements were also peppered with *shoulds* and *shouldn'ts*, especially, "You shouldn't talk about the family to others."

Intelligent and conversational, she never guessed that the underlying messages she actually gave her children were: "Don't trust anyone. Don't feel anything. Don't talk to anybody about what's going on in our family. Don't even talk to the family about the problems of the family." These weren't new rules. They had been handed down from Antony's father and his father's father. Anamarie served in her role to set up the perfect sick family system. Virtually closed off from the world, the system self-perpetuated the generational sickness that infected each of the Toscas' lives. They all looked good on the outside but were miserable on the inside. Everyone but John became a master at survival.

As each child grew, the facade of perfection grew thinner and thinner. John's death, the first glaring example of just how emotionally sick the family was, shattered the family image. In later years, each Tosca child developed problems that became obvious to the world, and even to Antony and Anamarie. It surprised both parents when their grown children demonstrated compulsive perfectionism, workaholism, insecurity, low self-esteem, a need to be "in control," and an inability to make decisions. One son followed his peers into drug abuse and addiction. A daughter silently became pregnant and left the family to have the baby and start another dysfunctional family to carry on the tradition. Each child eventually succumbed to the pressures of the outside world when his or her lack of an inside foundation took its toll.

Finally, coexisting in their unreal worlds of denial and isolation, Antony and Anamarie were forced to whisper the baffled battle cry of broken parents: "How have we failed?" They had created the model dysfunctional family. With no insight or emotional attachment, they had watched their children grow up and reap the seeds first sown many generations ago. One would have thought that after John's death they would have sought help so that the other children wouldn't experience the same pain. But the Toscas wouldn't discuss their problems with anyone. When they could have reached out, they did what most dysfunctional families do: They closed themselves off even further from the real world.

What Is a Dysfunctional Family?

Dysfunctional families are found throughout history and are recorded in the Bible. We have only to look in the book of Genesis at the first family to find troubled people so out of control that Cain ended up killing his brother, Abel. Lot slept with his daughters, meaning he did much more than just sleep with them. Jacob cheated his brother, Esau. And the house of David—the lineage of Christ—has many examples of dysfunction. David had sexual relations with a married woman and had her husband killed. Absalom rebelled against his father, David, and tried to take over the throne. Amnon raped his half sister, then Absalom murdered Amnon. It seems that David's lusts and self-destructive tendencies were passed down to his children, just as past sins infect families today when family members don't work through their problems. As in biblical times, unresolved problems are being reproduced and destroying a whole generation of kids.

Only recently have researchers come to understand the dynamics at work within self-perpetuating dysfunctional family systems. The first insights came from psychologists and social workers in the field of alcoholism. During the last 20 years, they saw certain patterns of behavior and relationships surface within families of alcoholics. They were surprised to discover that instead of confronting the alcoholics or placing them in a position to see the nature of their problems and making them accountable for their actions, family members "covered up" the problems and in other ways enabled the alcoholics to continue problem drinking.

Psychologists labeled those who enable the alcoholics to continue unchanged *codependents* and described their behavior as codependency. Although these terms have become popular buzzwords and are used to describe almost every ailment that exists, codependents are simply people who are dependent on other people who have problems. Codependents learn to survive as long as someone they are dependent on is attached to some other dependency, such as workaholism, alcoholism, or pornography. Codependents don't know how to exist when all is well, so they subconsciously work to keep things sick. They don't succeed, however. They merely survive until the people to whom they are attached become so sick that they must obtain help. Then the codependents are forced to change and often discover there are ways to exist beyond a mere survival mode.

Thus, those who are devoted to keeping alcoholics sick, for example, have codependent personalities and enable the addicts to continue their habits by covering up for them, offering excuses, and forbidding anyone in the family system to talk about the "family secret."

Codependents convince themselves that they are "stuck" and cannot change things, primarily because of their own fear of abandonment. Thus, they have an inappropriate tolerance of inappropriate behavior and often suffer from depression. Their goal is to control and contain family difficulties. In the process, they actually become hooked on controlling and containing. They wind up with as many problems as the alcoholics, only with symptoms that are much less visible. Those who initially appear to be saints tolerating abuse are actually scared little girls or boys struggling to survive.

When Steve started working with alcoholics in Texas in 1977, it didn't take long to see that it wasn't only the alcoholics who had problems. Most often, a typical alcoholic was married to a codependent, enabling wife who would do anything for him except what was needed to force him to change. She'd lie for him, cover up for him, and raise a sick family for him, but she wouldn't hold him accountable to get well.

Sometimes, for example, a boss would force an alcoholic employee into treatment. After a few days, if the alcoholic was not committed to recovery, he could hook his wife into believing that the boss had been unfair and the treatment was not needed. The entire staff would have to step aside and watch the wife take her husband out of the hospital, even though it meant he would be drunk again that night and would lose his job. It would be extremely rare to find a sick alcoholic married to a healthy spouse! A healthy spouse would have intervened or left long before the problem escalated to the point of needing treatment.

As the portrait of the family in an alcoholic home gradually emerged, psychologists began to identify nonalcoholic families with similar characteristics. They found traits of addictive/compulsive behavior, denial, workaholism, eating disorders, perfectionism, the need for power and control, and problems with expressing personal feelings and intimacy . . . but no alcohol. Family members in these homes acted out their lives in different roles, but the family members all had the same core characteristics that led them to grow up with a distorted view of others, themselves, and how to relate to the real world.

Roles That Are Played in Dysfunctional Families

Besides the basic physical needs of shelter, food, and clothing, all of us have emotional needs. In a healthy family system, the members as a unit provide one another with emotional comfort, safety, and security, and they instill feelings of self-esteem and self-worth while allowing room for autonomy and self-discovery.

Within a dysfunctional family system, however, members find that the whole family structure isn't meeting their basic psychological needs. Instead, needs are met by individual members, each of whom finds a different role to play to compensate for needs not met, instilled, or integrated by the family unit. The role isn't a true reflection of each person. Rather, the role engulfs each person who uses it as a means of survival. As family members' identities become wrapped up in their roles, the true individuals are lost until a major crisis may force the members to go back and try to retrieve what was left behind in childhood.

In a healthy family, one would normally find a group of people who are interdependent on each other. They are each unique, but because they honor the family and the relationships that exist there, they look to each other for support and help. They choose not to break from the family because it provides them with so much emotional and spiritual support. Life is easier for a person growing up in an interdependent family than it is for one growing up in a dysfunctional family.

Since the members of a dysfunctional family cannot trust each other, they rebel against relationships within the family. They replace interdependency with independence. Rejecting the identity of the family, they take on an independent identity outside it.

As you read the following descriptions of dysfunctional roles that children assume, see if you can discover which role you may have adopted in order to survive in your home. Keep in mind that everyone takes on a part of every role in a healthy family, because its members move in and out of roles as they choose. In a dysfunctional family, however, sick family members find themselves trapped in roles, unable to learn different ways to exist that would be far more rewarding.

The Lost Child

A lost child is a loner who frequently hangs out on the fringe of the group. If he or she has any friends at all, it is one or two others who also live like outcasts. A lost child is sad, feeling as if he or she doesn't belong anywhere. Often it takes a caring adult to take this child on as a special project in order to facilitate the child's becoming an active part of the group.

In a family, the lost child plays the role of "the different one" and functions on behalf of the family's need for autonomy and separateness. He or she may be physically separated by staying in the bedroom, or be separated mentally or spiritually by quietly pursuing different activities from the rest of the family, such as joining political causes or attending a different church. When parents think about this lost child, they think that he or she gives them no trouble.

These lost kids don't say much, don't ask much, and don't do much. They exist, making it through another day in painful loneliness. In a sense, they have made a statement with their lives. They have proclaimed that their families aren't healthy and that they choose not to participate. No one seems to notice them until some major catastrophe—such as pregnancy, running away, or suicide—jerks people back to the awareness that in isolation there must be a tremendous amount of pain.

Steve's brother Jerry was a lost child. He did everything beautifully—perfectly. He was never any trouble to anyone. Outside observers would have thought he was the perfect son. All of that made it even more difficult for his family when they discovered Jerry had not only been living with gay men, but he was also dying with AIDS. Sadly, as in Jerry's case, when parents discover how lost the child is, it is usually too late.

The Scapegoat

The role of the scapegoat child is to act out that which the rest of the family is feeling but not expressing. The scapegoat, most likely the "black sheep of the family," is often in trouble at school or with the law. Frequently, the scapegoat uses drugs.

The scapegoat provides the dysfunctional family with an "out," a way to focus attention away from themselves and their need to be responsible. "If only the scapegoat would get rid of his (or her) problem," family members might say, "then our family would be normal." The scapegoat child also represents the desire for help. He or she is screaming at the world through destructive behavior, begging for someone to notice that all is not well in the family and hoping that someone will intervene.

The teenagers who come into New Life Clinics for help are most often the family scapegoats. Sometimes they will be lost children, but usually they've assumed the role of troublemaker and have been involved with drugs and/or become so violent that their parents can no longer control them. When scapegoat teenagers come into our centers, they are each attached to one or two confused and troubled parents who hope their children can be fixed and returned to a normal behavioral state. Ironically, we often find these extremely troubled children to be the most rational members of their families. These children have unknowingly set up a crisis that forces Mom and Dad to get help. These "sacrificial lambs" place themselves on the altar of treatment in hopes that the sacrifice will be worthy of God's intervention and that their families might be saved. Frequently, the treatment provided the children is secondary to what must be done to solve their parents' problems.

The Clown/Distracter

Although this family member provides comic relief, there isn't much real humor in the way this child lives. The clown never shows pain or discomfort. If the emotions get too heavy, the distracter will provide a distraction so that heavy issues don't have to be faced, resolved, or confronted. The distracter's hidden message is, "Everything's fine. See, everyone is laughing. Why would you think something's wrong?" In effect, the clown/distracter provides a manifestation of the "denial" element for the family. Seething beneath the surface of the humor and laughter is intense anger that becomes a controlling force in this child's life.

Clown/distracter children from dysfunctional families often grow up to be immature and irresponsible. Never forced to grow up, they move frequently, run up big bills, and never hold a job for very long. Because they were allowed to laugh away their smaller problems, they have no idea how to solve the big problems that surface. If something is too big to make light of, they have learned the best thing to do is run. As adults, it's extremely painful for clown/ distracters to realize that they lack adult problem-solving skills because they never went through the pain of learning them as children. Although it's hard for these angry, hurting men and women to go back and grow up all over again, that's exactly what they must do.

This idea of going back and growing up all over again is often referred to as reparenting. In its most simple form, it is a resubmission to authority. Rather than continuing to make unhealthy, independent decisions, the adult clown instead makes a conscious choice to retract the boundaries to where they should have been when the person was an adolescent. It is a rather dramatic form of being mentored. Admitting that something is missing in the maturing process, the clown looks to someone else to temporarily train him in how to delay gratification and make solid decisions based on something other than emotions. As the person progresses, he takes more and more of his life back into his own hands. If successful, he emerges from the process with the moral sensitivity and wisdom needed to succeed outside the role of clown.

The Hero

This child tries to deal with pain by accomplishing good things for his or her family and for God. Some of what this child does is healthy; some isn't. A hero child assumes this role to survive. (This is the role each of us assumed.) It's a tough role because the child's self-expectations are so high. He or she also believes that everyone else's expectations are just as extreme.

The hero (or family savior) provides the family with self-esteem and accomplishment. The hero child is the one everyone can point to—the one who is "safe" to talk about, the one who often seems to have it "the most together." But the emotional burden of carrying the family standard is heavy. Thus, the hero is often the first one to break emotionally.

Like many today, both of us have experienced hero-related pressures that lead to burnout and superficial existence. Along the way, we've seen many others play out the hero role until the pressure becomes too great. Finally, the heroes crack under the stress. Ministries die. Families are destroyed. And children grow up to repeat the same unhealthy patterns. It's a burden to be a hero. If you are one, your lifelong challenge is to replace heroism with balance.

When one of Jim's family members received treatment for alcoholism, for instance, he quickly realized he wasn't the only one in ministry who had taken on the role of hero while growing up. There were several other ministers in the recovery group he attended for family members of alcoholics. Questions were piercing as each hero in the group was asked to look deeply at his motivation to work for God. It's hard to admit that sometimes what Christians do is a result of a need to survive, not the result of a pure motivation to serve God. Those of us who are family heroes have to deal with the question of motivation as we try to please God so that we can serve Him for healthy reasons rather than to compensate for an unhealthy past.

The Enabler/Doer

In this role, a child attempts to control everyone and everything in an effort to hold the family together, make it function (to the extent that it does), provide continuity, and smooth the rough spots. The doer is most often the oldest sibling (but may be a parent). Although probably feeling used and abused and unappreciated, the doer also enjoys the role of martyr and would rather function in this role and know what's expected than to face changes and an uncertain future. Other family members resent this person because he or she appears to have so much control. Yet the difficult situations never improve; the family doesn't get better.

This role particularly plagues Christians, so many of whom allow their families to be destroyed under the guise of servanthood or submission. It's tough to break through the denial of an enabler who believes that he or she is acting on Christian principles rather than on a sick survival mode. It's vital that enablers see the genuine fruits of their labor. It is one thing, for example, for an enabling person to stick by a spouse through good times and bad. It's something quite different when the enabler's actions actually cause the person being helped to experience more bad times than good.

We have both seen an entire ministry fall apart while the minister's faithful wife silently watched it happen. Whether in Philadelphia or Los Angeles, we've seen ministers' wives do all the wrong things for what they believe are the right motivations. If they could have seen what they were doing to themselves and the ministries by trying to smooth over problems, they might have spoken up and tried to implement positive changes. At least they might have admitted that all was not well.

If Anamarie Tosca, for instance, could have foreseen the impact her actions would have on her son, perhaps she wouldn't have allowed the family problems to flourish. Perhaps she would have been willing to break one of the unwritten rules that kept her and her children silent about just how serious the problems had become.

Rules in Dysfunctional Families

Just as individual members of dysfunctional families assume roles, a system of rules is also developed. These rules may be simple or complex, depending on whether abusive and/or addictive behavior is involved and whether there is a dysfunctional personality. But dysfunctional families all contain similar and very distinct traits and themes. You can use the following traits or statements that are regularly found in or used by dysfunctional families to evaluate your home or the home of someone you love.

Compulsive Behavior

Family members applying this rule always have to do something in a certain way, even when there's no logical or compelling reason to do so. (There may even be compelling reasons to do it differently.) It's a way one or more people try to manage their lives with a nice, orderly routine. But the compulsive person will fall apart if the routine is ever changed.

Constant Criticism

Even if it's well-meaning and done in love, perfectionism—and the criticism that results—is a trademark of a dysfunctional family. The best act or intention remains an open target for a remark that pierces through the deed to reveal its inadequacy. Every joke or jab becomes a clever means to express discontent or even anger over a family member's imperfection.

"You Should" or "You Shouldn't"

Although it's important to set boundaries and establish right and wrong, the words above often reflect perfectionistic and compulsive tendencies in the parents. A person raised under these harsh *shoulds* and *shouldn'ts* is frequently void of the moral foundations that answer "why." Rigidity frequently replaces his need to develop a rationale. There is no foundation for good decision making. One who grows up acting or reacting to *shoulds* and *shouldn'ts*, not knowing the reason, will naturally rebel against what was demanded and those who demanded it. This perfectionist, legalistic form of parenting is an extreme called "authoritarian parenting." Balance is the key that produces healthy kids who can make healthy choices.

"Don't Talk"

This phrase reflects the desire to keep family secrets. It is expressed as, "Keep the family honor," "Other people don't need to know about our problems," or "You shouldn't discuss our problems with other people."

An extreme example of this was a lady Steve met at a New Life Clinic. When she arrived, she didn't talk. No one could get through to her. She had learned the no-talk rule so well that she carried it into all her relationships. But as treatment progressed, the roots of that rule were slowly uncovered.

She remembered that when she was two, her father hanged her. She recalled choking for breath and her mother cutting her down moments before she would have died. Something so traumatic should have initiated help for her father, or at least her mother should have moved out to protect her little girl. Instead, everyone acted as if nothing was wrong—until the father burned down the house while his daughter was asleep in her crib. Her brother saved her with only seconds to spare. No wonder she wasn't talking when she came to us! She had learned that even the worst things are not worthy of discussion. Within three weeks of treatment, however, she was breaking her lifelong rule. There was nothing she wouldn't talk about with the staff and other patients.

It's too bad more people who have grown up with the no-talk rule can't have the same positive experience. Instead, they often live out their lives in painful isolation—unwittingly perpetuating the problem.

"Don't Feel"

Some family members are embarrassed to express emotions. Typically one parent in a dysfunctional family is absent emotionally. A common expression in such a family would be, "We know that our family loves one another; we just have difficulty expressing it." Or, "We're just not the type to be real demonstrative about it."

When Steve was a youth pastor in a small town, he met a troubled young girl who was not allowed to share her pain with her family. She also never received an open expression of love from her stoic father. No one knew how serious the problem was until she became pregnant. The love she couldn't feel from her father she had sought from boys. Desiring to hear "I love you," she had been willing to give up her standards, have sex, and feel like a tramp. What she ended up receiving was a baby girl—a candidate for another generation of pain.

"Don't Trust"

Members of a dysfunctional family have learned not to take anything at face value. Living with the quirks of at least one unpredictable personality and having to use associated dysfunctional behavior to adapt, immediate family members develop an uncanny ability to pick up on subtle behaviors and statements and "read" other people's intentions with amazing accuracy. They believe that what a person says has little to do with what he or she means.

We have seen this pattern develop in many families, especially when it becomes harder for them to make ends meet. The workaholic dad, for instance, who promises to be at the game but doesn't show up teaches his child not to trust. The mom who is so busy she forgets to pick up her daughter at school shows the child that trusting someone leads only to disappointment. Like other learned rules, this one is difficult to break.

Walking on Eggshells

When a family member responds unpredictably due to addiction, mood swings, or other reasons, the rest of the family never knows what to expect and feels obligated to accommodate the erratic behavior. Very quickly, the children take on responsibility for the troubled person's behavior, since they are usually blamed for any outbreak or disturbance. These future perfectionists live with the tyranny of the "if onlys," feeling that if only they were better, their mom or dad would stay in control and the situation would be better.

No Angry Words, Just Angry Behavior

The family members using this rule may even be proud of the fact that they never raise their voices or have arguments. However, terse or tense actions, avoidance, and withdrawal behavior typically reveal hostility and pent-up anger.

Children in this type of family learn never to ask if there's a problem because if there is, it's denied. (Anyone bold enough to suggest that there might be a problem is usually punished in an unrelated way for breaking the no-talk rule.)

When many or all of these rules are found in one family, it's a tough place for children (and their parents) to exist and attempt to have needs met. Family members become preoccupied with not breaking the rules, and one who doesn't adhere to the rules is either shamed or treated like an outcast. A child growing up in this type of home usually institutes the same kind of system when raising his or her own family. Instead of avoiding such rules, the adult uses them because that system is all the person knows—what he or she is comfortable with.

Aren't All Families Dysfunctional?

Before the 1990s, characteristics of dysfunctional families were seldom recognized. Today many people wonder if the concept of dysfunction isn't just another way of describing every family that has ever existed. "All families are dysfunctional," some say. "All children grow up with scars from unhealthy parents." As John and Linda Friel point out in their book on the subject, "Is it not true that almost everyone is codependent? Is it not true that almost everyone has some form of dysfunction in their childhood?"[1] We challenge this type of thinking, which is just a different way of denying the severity of family problems. Perhaps you are tempted to dismiss this material by saying, "Oh, all families are like this. Almost every family I know has one of these problems from time to time!" If so, be cautious. The danger is that this attitude often excuses a person from making needed changes that will prevent the next generation from having to experience the same types of problems.

"If everyone has 'it,'" someone else might ask, "doesn't dysfunction lose its conceptual and diagnostic meaning?" We don't think so, for the same reason that depression has not lost its meaning despite the fact that everyone has "it" at one time or another over a lifetime. *The Diagnostic and Statistical Manual of Mental Disorders of the American Psychiatric Association* "always describes symptoms, but asks us to look at length and severity of symptoms." Year after year, a truly dysfunctional family will experience worsening problems with no hope of the situation improving.

Indeed, all families have plenty of problems, but this doesn't make them dysfunctional. Family members may lie to each other from time to time and resort to other unhealthy behaviors, but they aren't, in the clinical sense, dysfunctional because they don't use inappropriate adaptations as a way of life. Parents in these families aren't perfect, but they somehow find a way of connecting with their children rather than unknowingly trapping them. These parents provide their children with values, self-worth, and confidence. Their faith in God strengthens their children rather than leaving them feeling guilty or inadequate. Parents in families where there's a normal amount of unhealthy behavior don't fit the label of dysfunctional, for they somehow guide their children and allow them to develop into healthy adults who are free of tremendous emotional baggage from childhood.

Some families could actually be classified as healthy! When John Tosca died, his brothers and sisters were forced to face the reality that something was terribly wrong with their family. But they still had no idea what it would be like to be in a family where things were basically all right. Not until they attended college did they discover that other families had found ways to succeed. They discovered what it was like for family members to communicate and share feelings with one another.

Brigette Tosca's best friend in college also came from a large family that had problems ranging from an anorexic sister to a brother who was caught shoplifting. But Brigette found that communication patterns in her friend's family were entirely different from those in her own. There was an openness of emotional expression and accountability to one another. Family members weren't afraid to talk about their feelings, to be intimate and emotionally honest, and to make one another feel wanted, necessary, and needed when they weren't involved in normal family arguments. Brigette marveled at how her friend talked with her mother on the phone as if they were close friends. They were, in the truest sense, friends, something Brigette had never experienced with her own mother. In healthy families, children and their parents eventually become friends. Children don't spend their lives alienated from their parents.

Adult Children of Dysfunctional Families

As we've seen, children who are raised in dysfunctional homes grow up to have problems, many of them severe. These people often have a bad case of the "overs." They overachieve, overwork, overexercise, overspend, and "overtry." They operate on what could be described as a "try-hard" battery, believing that a little more effort will produce the radical and positive changes that have eluded their families. Yet adult children from dysfunctional homes often can't identify their problems and make sense of their insecurities and compulsive behaviors. Children who come out of dysfunctional families grow up in pain. There is always that gnawing sense that something isn't right, but they're unable to discover their problems and resolve them. Often these adults believe they are unique—the only ones who have felt the way they do.

In recent years, however, as counselors better understood the traits and behavioral patterns of dysfunctional families, these adult children have found some relief in identifying with others who come from similar homes. The label "adult children of dysfunctional families" has become a rallying point for their own mental health. Frequently, they are greatly relieved to discover that they're not alone, that thousands of others have grown up in dysfunctional homes and exhibit similar feelings and behaviors.

The following characteristics are common in most adult children from dysfunctional families. If you have wondered whether you come from a dysfunctional home, perhaps this list will help you determine your past so you can make decisions about your future.

In most adult children of dysfunctional families:

1. Major chunks of their childhood memories have been blocked out.

2. They have had to guess at what is normal behavior because they have seen so few examples of it.

3. They grew up feeling they were different from others, that others have been given great insights into how to live, but they haven't acquired the same knowledge.

4. They judge themselves unmercifully, never feeling they measure up to their parents' demands or God's expectations. Most of the time, they simply feel bad and apologetic about being themselves.

5. They have difficulty having fun. To let loose is to jeopardize control, and that feels intolerable. They take themselves and life in general very seriously.

6. They find it hard to follow a project through to its end, usually becoming distracted and thereby sabotaging the end result.

7. Because they lived in a fake world and were forced to project a false image of their families, they find it just as easy to tell a lie as to tell the truth, especially if it makes them or someone else look or feel better.

8. They constantly seek approval and affirmation. Their need for attention can often overwhelm those around them.

9. They find themselves at one end of two extremes, being either super-responsible or super-irresponsible.

10. They consider much of their behavior to be self-defeating.

11. They are loyal people, even when evidence doesn't support their loyalty.

12. They are compulsive, but their compulsiveness is often more positive in appearance than that of their parents.

As these characteristics suggest, adult children of dysfunctional families are seldom happy. In fact, they are often miserable—full of fear, depression, and anxiety. They may complain about everyone and everything in a futile effort to take the focus off their inadequacies. They often possess what could be called the "miserable-personality syndrome" because they view existence as nothing but a living hell that's full of internal torment from invisible critics who exist only in their minds.

Although adults from dysfunctional families are able to deny the severity of their problems, their inadequate choices of how to survive eventually give way to some type of personal crisis or disaster. If this crisis doesn't provide them with the opportunity to seek help and change, they may perpetuate their problems through inadequate communication skills and emotional distancing. This leads directly, in turn, to a new generation of children who grow up with little or no sense of self-worth or self-esteem. Having had no parents who instilled a foundation of value within them, they seek approval from peers at any cost—even at the cost of their souls.

We have begun with the topic of dysfunctional families because of the impact that sick families have on children and society as a whole. As you'll see in ensuing chapters, kids who are most at risk come from troubled homes, have low self-worth and/or low self-esteem, cling to unhealthy peer groups, and succumb to the groups' destructive influences. Even kids from what appear to be good, stable, Christian homes will experience low self-esteem if communication and behavioral patterns that exist in their households cut off the children emotionally and leave them struggling to survive.

Even if you and your spouse are well-intentioned, conscientious parents, this doesn't provide immunity from problems for you or your family. On the other hand, if many of the traits, problems, and personalities described in this chapter are familiar to you and your family, there's hope! The sickest individuals are so deeply rooted in denial that they can't identify their problems. If you've broken through that wall of denial and can see that changes need to occur within you, your resolve can be the beginning of incredible change in your life and family. Family members who decide to move toward positive changes will find themselves liberated from many family "secrets" and free to stand on their own feet. Those who start to recover from dysfunction will begin to positively influence the rest of the family because they will no longer "play the game" or feel compelled to stay in family "roles."

You Can Make a Difference

If you're convinced that you grew up in a dysfunctional home and may be re-creating some of the same problems in your current family, relax! Many Christians feel this way. Fortunately, you can take steps to ensure that your children won't have to suffer for some of the mistakes you, your parents, and your grandparents have made. You can help your children become part of the "transitional" generation that takes bold steps toward healthy relationships.

Talk Openly with Your Children

First, take time to talk with your kids. Honestly tell them what your childhood was like. Admit the mistakes you've made. Assure your children that you will attempt to do better. Be willing to express your feelings with them. Explore their feelings; listen to what they're saying and what they might be trying to communicate.

Build Trust

Another important step is to build trust with your children. Be a person of your word. Let them know that only a rare exception could cause you to not be with them when you've promised to be there. Kids know that sometimes things don't work out. They understand the rare exception. Let your behavior in all areas be consistent so they don't have to be afraid of setting you off or take the blame when you're out of control.

Consider Counseling

Most important, realize that an objective counselor can save you and your children years of grief and dramatically speed up your recovery. It's almost impossible for any of us to work out deep problems of dysfunction on our own. If your behavior is not honoring God, humble yourself enough to consult with someone qualified to perceive the real foundation and motivation of your actions. Your commitment to counseling may be the key to saving your family from further pain.

The family unit is the most vital institution in existence. The future of each of our families—and our society—depends on our confronting dysfunction and raising our children in a healthy environment of support that is founded on an active belief in God. If we faithfully do what is within our power to do, God will faithfully do what is beyond our capabilities. Our job is to trust Him and raise our children according to His principles. But God cannot work with denial. We must be willing to face the reality of our difficult situations and work toward resolving problems that will otherwise inflict some of the misery we've experienced on our children.

We must cling to one piece of wisdom: Life makes sense. Children don't become involved with drugs by accident. It is not an unsolvable mystery why children rebel and pursue promiscuity. They are rebelling against dysfunctional relationships, not principles. If we can restore the relationships, we can save our children from all sorts of destruction. There are answers to why we "lose" our children and solutions to how we can retrieve them. They are not easy answers, but they exist. We hope you'll find many of them in the following pages as you discover how children are trapped and how we parents can help them once again run free.

CHAPTER THREE

The Transitional Generation

A deep sadness filled Mary's eyes, and Dave had that worried look. They had been through the wringer. Illness, work pressures, relationship problems, financial stress, and raising two pre-schoolers had made the year difficult. Sure, they had made it through another year—like always. But this year had brought on more stress and depression than previous years. As they sat in bed discussing their problems one evening, Mary began to cry softly. Dave figured the tears resulted from one of the many tensions in the family until she blurted out, "I wish I had a mom to hold me and take care of me."

Dave's eyes welled up with tears, too. "I wish we both had a mom to give us encouragement and attention."

Dave and Mary are not unique. In fact, we believe

they are in the majority. Like others who are trying to be "parents of the year," they practice the incredible juggling act of trying to keep everything going in the right direction, and they receive little, if any, help from other family members, especially their parents. Dave and Mary are also from typically dysfunctional families. Dave is the adult child of an alcoholic, and Mary's family is just plain strange. Both of them were family heroes who excelled while other family members used their anger and energy for destructive purposes.

During college and their early years of marriage, they hardly noticed the lack of family support. After all, they had no standard for evaluating what is normal. But as years passed and they became more needy, Dave and Mary realized they seldom received support from their parents. Being the only Christians in their families made it hard for them to share deeply with other family members who had different lifestyles.

What are the answers? Is it possible for Dave and Mary to receive the parental support they need? What about their two precious children? Will those kids inherit the same struggles because they were born into the chain of a dysfunctional family?

Dave and Mary can become the transitional generation in their families. They can break the chains of dysfunction and bring hope and new life to their children. Will it be easy? No. Will it be worth making the changes? Without a doubt, the answer is yes! The apostle Paul gave all of us a good piece of advice: "Be very careful, then, how you live—not as unwise but as wise" (Eph. 5:15). With that verse in mind, let's see what we parents must do to become the transitional generation.

Look at Yourself

The first step is to discover who you are. Much of your life will be the result of good or bad choices. If you come from a dysfunctional family, you'll need to better understand why you act the way you do before you can make wise choices. The more you understand yourself, the easier it will be to make the right choices for yourself and your family. Let's look at some general characteristics that often apply to adult children of dysfunctional homes. Perhaps not all of them will apply to you, but they will provide valuable insights.

What Is Normal?

If you're from a dysfunctional family, feeling different and somewhat isolated is probably part of your personal makeup. Most of your life, you've received double messages, such as: "I love you; don't bother me. Always tell the truth; your father just had a bad day at the office. You are smart; don't be an idiot." How can all of this make sense to a person? Which part do you believe? Chances are you probably believed both messages and were confused.

One friend of ours, raised with alcoholic parents, is always asking: "What is a normal feeling or reaction to this problem?" All his life he has had to guess what's normal.

Another friend described his relationship with his family of origin this way: "Either I'm crazy and they're all normal, or I'm normal and they're all crazy." Who's right and who's wrong? Anyone from a dysfunctional family struggles to know what is normal.

When I Relax I Feel Guilty

Carol Ann worked from morning until night without ever taking a break. She read the Bible while vacuuming. When she was sick, she felt so guilty that she usually got up from bed too soon and delayed the healing process. She was the most dependable Sunday school teacher, volunteered at her son's school, participated in three Bible studies, managed the girls' soccer team, and never missed her exercise class. Mother of the year? Probably. Wife of the century? Most of the time. The finest teacher and coach in the city? You bet. But all wasn't well. Although involved in many activities, she had few friends and seldom, if ever, stopped to enjoy life and smell the roses.

Finally, Carol Ann's body began to fall apart. She had taken life so seriously that her body simply shut down. It was the only way it could get relief. Thankfully, she began a healthy relationship with a wise counselor, who helped her relax and enjoy life before it was too late.

Carol Ann came from an emotionally abusive family. Somewhere along the way, she adapted to her pain by taking life too seriously. Like many people from dysfunctional families, she tended to judge herself without mercy. Rather than responding as most people do to negative family issues by being irresponsible, however, Carol Ann overcompensated and became extremely responsible.

Am I Having Fun Yet?

Innocent children know how to have fun. As adults, it's often the child within us who has fun and knows how to play. Because Carol Ann's child within had been repressed for so long, it needed to be discovered and developed. Carol Ann needed permission to be the child she never was. She now understands that because her parents were in such great pain, she grew up fast and missed most of her childhood.

What's she doing to catch up with her inner child? Her prescription for wholeness and health is to relax and do nothing. Ironically, Carol Ann had to plan times of spontaneity at first. She is learning to take time for herself without deciding that each minute of every day has to be productive. You, too, may have to follow Carol Ann's prescription for happiness.

When Is Loyalty Harmful?

Since many adults from dysfunctional families don't really understand what normal behavior is, they find themselves putting up with abuse. If people with whom you're involved aren't treating you properly, it's important to rethink your loyalty. In itself, loyalty is an admirable quality. But carried to an extreme, it may be harmful, as the following illustration shows.

Janet's boss was obnoxious, rude, and demanded more hours and energy than were appropriate. Because her first husband had been a tyrant and her alcoholic father was far from compassionate, Janet had never learned that she deserved fair treatment. So she'd bite her lip and press on. Finally, other women in her department started mentioning that she was being treated unfairly, and she began to think about the inconsistencies. Then she made the best and smartest move she could have made. She confronted her boss and eventually changed jobs. She felt false guilt for a while, but now she's much happier.

Perhaps, because of undeserved loyalty, you are hooked in a relationship or situation that's not good for you. Perhaps, if you can be easily manipulated by guilt, you think you owe something to the person who is mistreating you. Stop and re-evaluate. Loyalty is a strength, but it can damage your emotional, spiritual, physical, and family life.

Difficulty with Intimacy

If you come from a dysfunctional family, there's probably nothing more desirable to you than having a healthy, intimate relationship. However, difficulty with intimacy shows up in most adults from dysfunctional families. Why? The most obvious reason is that you have no frame of reference for a healthy, intimate relationship because you probably never saw one up close. Parents are models, whether they want to be or not. When it comes to developing a loving parent-child relationship with their own children, for example, many adult children of dysfunctional families carry with them only the experience of inconsistency—having felt loved one day and rejected the next.

This leads to difficulty in being vulnerable. If we fear giving ourselves freely and wholly to another, we will not achieve emotional or spiritual intimacy with that person. The fears that come from our dysfunctional relationships with our parents will infect our relationships with our spouses, our children, and our friends.

I'm Not Okay, and That's Not Okay

Remember the popular phrase of the early 1970s "I'm okay, you're okay"? Books were written about it. Tapes, films, and teachers expanded on it. Why? We think it was because so many people felt bad about themselves. They looked inward and saw failure. They suffered from a poor view of themselves and tried to grab anything that would help. Adults from dysfunctional families commonly suffer from low self-esteem.

Tom, for instance, looks as if he has everything going for him. Intelligent and witty, he has a good job and a nice family. Yet he feels isolated and unloved, and he often becomes unlovable. He is easily discouraged, anxious, and often depressed. Why? He is so preoccupied with self-consciousness that his capacity for fulfillment is easily destroyed. In families like the one in which he was raised, low self-esteem is the norm. His mom and dad divorced when he was eight, and his father seldom visited. His mom tried to be a good parent but didn't give Tom the emotional or physical attention he needed. So as an adult, he tried to dull his pain with alcohol, fancy cars, exotic vacations, nice clothes, and other materialistic trappings. He sought ways to find the approval and affirmation he desperately wanted from home but had seldom received. He viewed himself as different and tried to compensate with things and toys. It didn't work.

Was it Tom's fault that his parents got a divorce? Did he have anything to do with the fact that his father seldom showed him any attention? No. But most people from dysfunctional families nevertheless suffer from a low self-image and spend their lives overcompensating.

You Can Make a Difference

If you strongly identified with the previously mentioned characteristics, there's hope! With God's help, you can change. Most important, your children don't have to suffer the same pain you have endured. You may be loving them more than you've ever loved them before, but sometimes love is not enough.

You can work on the problem areas until you resolve them. You can break the chains of family dysfunction and become the transitional generation. Are you up to the challenge?

Recognize the Need for Help

Many pastors and youth workers with whom we relate are from less-than-perfect homes. In fact, more and more younger church workers are the "heroes" of dysfunctional families who must now deal with dysfunction in their own marriages. One pastor told us:

> Life in my family was miserable. We were falling into negative patterns of communication, and it was getting worse each month. I tried changing my wife's behavior, switching jobs, and preaching to the kids. Then it finally dawned on me that I could get help for myself. It has been the best possible experience for my life, my marriage, my ministry, and my children. Life still isn't perfect. I learned it never will be. In counseling, I learned some tools that have helped me cope with my past and my present situations. Why did I wait so long?

Why do too many of us wait so long to get help? If your spouse or children won't seek help, what's keeping you from doing so?

We play golf. (Actually, we *attempt* to play golf.) The other day, Jim was discussing the fact that when he took lessons, his golf game became worse for a while before it improved. Basically, he had progressed as far as possible with his unorthodox swing. A teaching professional helped him understand why his golf shots weren't working and how he could develop a proper swing to correct many of his problems.

The first time out on the course after his lessons, Jim shot 10 strokes worse than before. Needless to say, he almost gave up. Having been taught the skills to determine what needed to be corrected, he concluded he was doing almost *everything* wrong. However, he kept working on the lessons. Today, we're happy to announce that he is almost not a duffer. Hardly pro material, but he's on his way to a more enjoyable game.

Likewise, sometimes pain comes before freedom. Don't wait until life becomes impossible. Seek the help of a trusted counselor, friend, pastor, or relative before your issues become too complicated. Someone once put it this way: "If you aren't growing, you're dying!"

A variation on that statement that we parents must keep in mind is, "If it's easy for you to be a parent, you may not be parenting." Parenting is tough work. You need to be a trainer, coach, guide, counselor, and leader. None of this is accomplished free of pain.

Get Counseling

Usually the parents who could most benefit from a counselor in terms of dealing with deep-rooted resentment, anger, or other emotions have too much pride to allow themselves to ask for such help. One of the healthiest, "freeing" decisions you can make is to meet with a dedicated and qualified family counselor if you and your family have communication-related difficulties or if you recognize even more severe problems.

Whatever problems exist for you and/or your spouse—and ultimately for your children—it's important to remember that the problems didn't develop overnight or even during a week. What took many months and years to develop may require at least as much time to unravel. Although counseling may seem to be a long, arduous process, take heart in the realization that it's an easy and healthy solution compared to the progression of untreated problems or issues. You—and hopefully members of your family—must be willing to expend as much energy and time solving the problems as the family did in maintaining them.

Some problems are significant enough to cause problems not only for you, but also for your spouse and family. If you know or even suspect that you may have a problem in one of the following areas, don't hesitate to seek counseling. Likewise, if one of your children has a problem in one of these areas— whether or not he or she recognizes it or is ready to admit it—consider family counseling.

- Sexual abuse—whether you were a victim or a perpetrator
- Sexual addiction
- Alcoholism
- Drug abuse
- Drug addiction
- Depression
- Anxiety

Whether or not the person(s) with the problem is willing to seek help, the rest of the family should seek counseling anyway. As other family members start to take responsibility and deal with their problems, the unhealthy person(s) will have a greater and quicker chance for recovery.

Counseling is seldom a quick, shot-in-the-arm, one-time treatment. It can't replace friendships, family, or the church. It should never veer a person away from solid biblical principles. It is a process of uncovering and unraveling, seeing possibilities, and viewing information in a new light. In counseling, the counselor brings family problems out for open discussion. Instead of being covered up, glossed over, or minimized, problems are presented as they really are, allowing family members to confront the issues and their underlying emotions.

The most valuable component of counseling is that it provides the family with an objective observer who is emotionally detached from the problems and can guide the family toward healthier alternatives and healing.

Seek Support

Like Dave and Mary, who wished they had a mother who would hold, nurture, and care for them, far too many adults today haven't developed a personal support system. In 1940, more than 70 percent of American homes had at least one resident grandparent. Today that figure is less than 2 percent. In our mobile society, the extended family is not as available, and for many people from broken families, it's not an option anyway.

All of us must find and be a part of support

systems. If parents are not in some sort of support system, we highly question the long-term foundation of their primary relationships with God, spouse, children, and friends. God created all of us with a need to give and receive support, and yet many of us feel and act like isolated islands. We believe that support is needed in four different areas:

1. Mentors
2. Mutual support
3. Influencing others
4. Personal relationship with God

Mentors. Do you have at least one mentor? Is there someone whose example you can follow when it comes to parenting decisions, lifestyle issues, and Christian beliefs? We need mentors in the parenting world just like in the business world. We all need an apprenticeship. We all need the input of more mature, wise, experienced persons.

No one these days wears a sandwich board that reads, "I want to be your mentor." (If someone did, it'd be easy to suspect motives.) You must find a mentor. Often older saints in church are filled with gems of wisdom. Several years ago, Jim asked an older pastor to have lunch with him. Their discussion developed into a weekly lunch meeting for more than three years. What an opportunity for learning through someone else's experiences!

Mutual support. The healthiest people have found mutual support systems. Our systems have been weekly support groups and home Bible studies connected with our church. For others, mutual support systems may be a mom's-day-out club, tennis-and-lunch club, book-a-month club, sports activities, classes, and so on.

Families need to find a support system, too. Far too many of them have little relationship with others passing through the same seasons of life. We believe God's plan is for families to feel a sense of belonging within their community.

To use a personal illustration, one of Jim and Cathy's daughters was born with a serious heart condition. Their support group from church supplied the turkey dinner at Thanksgiving, prepared meals for six weeks, cleaned the house, baby-sat, offered prayers, took our family out to dinner, and helped us go through a time that was basically a blur. Friendships deepened even through the tough times.

Likewise, Steve and Sandy receive lots of help through a "parents' growth group" at church. Weekly discussions deal with parenting issues, but it's amazing how often these issues go back to the couples' feelings of inadequacy. Several parents in the group will talk about what a miserable day they've had and what they perceive to be a dismal failure with one of their kids. Suddenly, everybody laughs because they can all relate, and the vulnerability and openness of the group help everyone.

As you've already gathered, we believe that a vibrant church can provide great opportunities for mutual support. However, we'd quickly add that we've never found a perfect church. Every church has foibles, troubles, and traumas. However, we can't think of a better place for you and your family to work on being the transitional generation. We urge you to find a fellowship where love and grace abound, one that will encourage you in your vertical relationship with God and in your horizontal relationships with other strugglers in the faith.

A friend of ours named Anne is a real inspiration. At age 35, she was an extremely successful businesswoman living along the Southern California coast. But as a young girl, Anne had been sexually abused by a relative. To cover her pain, she withdrew from church, resented God, and put all her energy into building a successful career. She accomplished her objectives but found life to be increasingly empty.

One Sunday morning, Anne met an older woman while taking a morning jog along the beach. They struck up a strong friendship, and the woman invited Anne to church. Anne laughed and said, "Thanks, but I'm not a believer, and I'm not interested." But when Anne returned to her condo, to her own surprise, she took a shower, dressed up, and drove directly to her new friend's church. In the parking lot, she asked herself, *Why did I come?*

Nevertheless, at church that day Anne found a group of people who had a zeal for life and a vibrant faith in God. She kept coming back. She met other women who had been abused and whose faith was helping them deal with their pain. She met singles who really enjoyed life and were different from the singles-bar crowd she socialized with but didn't really like.

Eventually, Anne made a commitment to Christ and even started working with the youth group. Her radiant personality, energy, and love of life attracted kids in the group toward her. One evening, she told her story of abuse and how she had received personal healing through a relationship with God. The kids sat in stunned silence. When she finished speaking, girls crowded around her. Now she has a wonderful counseling ministry with young people, a dynamic faith in God, positive Christian friends, and a church home where she feels loved and cared for and can connect with others.

Today, there are thousands of wonderful churches in which God is alive and life is meaningful. If you don't participate regularly in a religious fellowship, you're missing an important part of life.

Influence others. Another form of support takes place when you influence others. Through the years, both of us and our spouses have chosen to invite people to live in our homes. It might be an unwed mother or a seminary student who needs a place to stay during a difficult time. These have often been positive times of mentoring and influence. Again, we aren't walking around with the word *mentor* on our business cards, but we've found that a part of our ministry is in helping others learn from our experiences—both our failures and our victories.

How is your support system? If it's weak, don't

wait for someone to come to you. You may have to wait a lifetime. Ask someone to lunch, or invite him or her over for dessert. Take the initiative. Be proactive. Find a positive support base. It's out there but will probably require some work and time to locate it. Who can you call today?

Seek a personal relationship with God. A phenomenal experience took place when Jesus taught His disciples to pray. In the Sermon on the Mount, Jesus said, "This, then, is how you should pray: 'Our Father in heaven, hallowed be your name' " (Matt. 6:9). Although the Lord's Prayer is very familiar to most Christians, there's a chance the early disciples didn't hear anything after the first sentence. Perhaps Jesus had to repeat the prayer. Why? They couldn't get past the first two words: *Our Father.* This phrase seems normal enough today, but it wasn't for Jews living in Jerusalem at the time of Christ. God was called *Yahweh*, which means "I am that I am." To the Jews, God was so impersonal and powerful that He didn't have a personal name. Then Jesus came along and called God *Abba*, which means "Daddy." Two thousand years ago in Israel, one of the first words a child would learn was *Abba*. See the significance? Jesus called God Abba. It was an endearing name. Jesus radically changed our approach to God. He personalized it.

Maybe you've come from a dysfunctional family where your earthly father was not all you had hoped he would be. If you haven't already, you can come to the heavenly Father—Abba—who will reassure you of His deep love. God cares more about your wholeness and the health of your family than you do. After all, He created you and wants you to be at peace and fulfilled.

Do we sound a little preachy? Perhaps we are. But when we see people really thriving in their lives and families, it is often because they're not doing it alone but are depending on the power of God.

CHAPTER FOUR

Growing Up at Risk

I must look like everybody else.

—Christie, age 12

I have no idea how to relate to my children's generation. Everything moves so fast, and I'm scared to death. Really, I'm paralyzed, so I don't do anything. I feel as if I'm a casual observer in the raising of my children.

—Christie's mother, age 41

The atmosphere in Jim's office was tense. Leesa and her mother, both exceptionally pretty, obviously were frustrated with each other. Leesa sat as far from her mother as possible. Jim started his counseling session by simply asking, "Who wants to go first?"

Before Leesa could open her mouth, her mother blurted out, "Leesa is being a slut. She sleeps with her boyfriend. She drinks at parties, watches raunchy movies, and now she expects me to allow her to sleep in the same room with her boyfriend on our ski trip."

When Leesa finally spoke, her eyes were moist and focused on the floor. Her response surprised Jim. "But Mom, I'm only imitating you since you left Dad. I don't do anything you don't do. You live one life here at the church and an entirely different life when you drive out of the parking lot."

Ouch! Those words were a direct hit. Leesa's mother started to cry, and in a meek defense she said, "We're not here to talk about me. We're here to talk about you!"

Like many young people, Leesa is growing up in a generation at risk. Life for her and her mother is not "The Cosby Show." Leesa's main problem is a troubled relationship with her mom. In her case, this troubled relationship affects her more than some of the issues with which other teens struggle. Every day, Leesa and her mom, like most people, make difficult decisions in a life that isn't exactly what they had planned. It's a tough world out there—tougher still for today's youth. Problems such as drug addiction, teenage pregnancy, dropping out of school, suicide, and peer pressure all weigh heavily on the minds of our young people. For many parents, pastors, teachers, and civic leaders, these issues pose dilemmas that must be grappled with daily. There are no easy answers. There are, however, several options we parents can choose to reduce the negative risk factors in our lives and those of our children. But first, let's make sure we understand some of the incredibly difficult issues influencing our kids.

The Troubled Journey

Today's kids live in a media-bombarded generation. If it's not MTV, it's movies. If it's not movies, then it's the average four hours a day of rock music they listen to. If it's not music, it's the good ol' television, except television isn't what it used to be. The average teenager is able to watch 14,000 simulated acts of intercourse or innuendo to intercourse on prime-time programs. Many of today's young people are hooked on soap operas. Recently, during a speech at a high school assembly, Jim asked the teenagers how they liked soap operas. Soaps got a standing ovation! Do soaps influence this generation of young people? Of course they do, and people who aren't married to each other engage in 94 percent of the acts of intercourse or suggestions of sex on those soaps.

The MTV Generation?

Most parents have heard of MTV, but few bother to actually view it. That's not true for this generation of teenagers. The average teenager watches 10 hours of MTV a week, compared to spending 1.4 hours a week at church. MTV is more than a music channel. In the words of Robert Pittman, former president and chief executive officer of MTV, "Early on, we made a key decision that we would be the voice of young America. We were building more than just a channel; we were building a culture." [1]

Not only does MTV play music videos throughout the day, but it also dictates fashion and dance trends. "Our goal," Pittman said, "is to make MTV the leading authority on young adult culture—worldwide." Unfortunately, the heroes of this generation of teens are not in church, nor are they athletes or police officers. The heroes are MTV superstars. Yet even this generation's most popular female vocalist, Madonna, said this about her peers: "The actors and singers and entertainers I know are emotional cripples. Really healthy people aren't in this business, let's face it." [2]

MTV in a Nutshell:

- About 55.4 million homes in the United States are wired to receive MTV.
- Forty countries—including Argentina, Hungary, and Japan—tune in to MTV. When Asia gets hooked up, MTV will add 33 more countries to its audience.
- MTV has changed the way advertising works. For example, a 28-second commercial for McDonald's breakfast burrito has 37 different images. That, of course, is faster than one image per second.
- Within 10 years, MTV has aired about eight thousand different music videos. Madonna and Rod Stewart have made the most. Each has created 36 music videos during those 10 years—about one every three and a half months.
- A group's music video that appears three times during MTV's "120 Minutes" show will be seen by more people than the total number of fans who show up for the same group's three-week concert tour.
- In 1993, MTV began transmitting three channels simultaneously. One channel looks like traditional MTV. The other two channels each specialize in a certain music genre.

- MTV's plans for the future include Rockplexxes, which are really "amusement mall/television studios" open to the public.[3]

Parenting this generation of kids isn't easy. Parents are often disturbed to find their children spending valuable time and hard-earned money on activities and products that contradict biblical principles. For example, some young people devote hours listening to the wrong kinds of music. Rock expert Al Menconi believes that rock music meets three of kids' most basic needs:

1. The rock star (via tapes, compact discs, and videos) spends huge amounts of time with the young people—providing companionship.
2. The rock star accepts the kids as they are—providing acceptance.
3. The rock star relates to the young people's problems—providing identification.[4]

Fulfilling the needs of companionship, acceptance, and identification is first and foremost the task of parents. When we parents fail, our young people fill that void with something or someone else. Therefore, any time we spend with our children is time wisely invested.

Search Institute in Minneapolis, Minnesota, recently released a report on America's teenagers titled "The Troubled Journey: A Portrait of 6th to 12th Grade Youth." In surveying 46,799 kids, Search Institute discovered that 90 percent of them fail to meet standards for "well-being." Also, nine out of 10 of those kids had more negative factors working against them than positive factors working for them. Those figures mean that almost all kids are in danger of slipping into such risky behavior as premarital sex, reckless driving, drug abuse, or eating disorders.

We were extremely interested in this study because it set out to discover why some kids mature into healthy, responsible adults and others don't. Researchers found that an alarmingly high percentage of kids show signs of at-risk behavior because they:

- are alone at home. Fifty-eight percent spend two hours or more each day at home without adult supervision.
- have hedonistic values. Forty-eight percent hold self-serving values such as "having lots of money," "having lots of fun and good times," and "being popular and well liked."
- watch too much television. Forty percent watch three or more hours of television each day.
- go to drinking parties. Thirty-one percent frequently attend parties where alcohol is served. This percentage jumps to 61 percent of high school seniors.
- feel stressed. Twenty-one percent feel stressed about their life most of the time. It's not easy to be a teenager or preteen.[5]

Additional Risk Factors

Today, the number of AIDS cases among teenagers is doubling every 14 months. Although there are seven infected men for every infected woman, the ratio drops to three to one among urban teens. The founder of our nation's first adolescent AIDS clinics in the Bronx says that now a "far greater number of cases are spread by heterosexual sex."

Another major factor that causes young people to be at risk is the disintegration of the family unit. No one has a perfect family. Few, if any, families experience no struggles. However, parents must be aware of what's taking place within their families. Much of the national debate about family decline tacitly assumes that family disintegration is primarily due to women's roles, choices, and responsibilities. But this assumption overlooks what may be the single most troubling family trend of our era: male flight from family life.

According to the *Chemical People* newsletter, approximately one of every four children in the United States today—about 15 million—is growing up without a father in the house. That's more than twice as many as in 1960. A study at the University of Pennsylvania found that:

- More than half of these 15 million children have never visited their fathers' homes.
- More than 40 percent don't see their fathers at all in a typical year.
- Only one in six children sees his or her father an average of once or more per week.[6]

A Reason for Hope

There's no doubt that life is tough out there for young people and that risk factors are present.

However, many kids and their families are doing well in spite of the challenges. They are depositing healthy decisions into their emotional, spiritual, and family bank accounts. Lorna, for instance, has been raising three teenagers basically on her own. Her husband has been out of the home for several years and periodically returns on a holiday or his own birthday. Despite the odds being stacked against them, Lorna and her children are thriving. Life isn't easy for them, but she's doing an excellent job of parenting on purpose and preventing risky behavior in her children.

Lorna has made some wise decisions, such as:

- ongoing church involvement.
- lowering her financial stress by living below her means.
- planning that the family eats together at least four nights a week.
- expecting each child to do household chores and all homework.
- taking vacations together and at least once every three months going on a special weekend outing—usually camping, because of limited finances.
- encouraging her children to be involved in school activities and attending school events whenever possible.
- exercising at least three days a week and hardly ever missing an adult Bible study on Tuesday nights.

You Can Make a Difference

Even though kids are in crisis and the risk factors appear to be a given, let's look together at major "assets" that will help reduce kids' at-risk behaviors.

Set Parental Standards

Developing parental standards is not the only factor in deterring at-risk behavior, but it's one of the most important. Often, kids who do well know what behavior their parents expect of them and the consequences of inappropriate behavior. We have found that homes in which parents have set standards and have discussed them ahead of time with their children are the healthiest and experience the least rebellion. Kids want to know what's expected of them. If your children don't know their boundaries, they don't know whether they are violating the family rules. Consistency is a key. If you lovingly discipline your kids and provide consequences for violating family rules, the odds are your children will have few serious behavioral problems.

Another vital parenting standard for healthy relationships is monitoring. When each of your children leaves the house, simply knowing where he or she is going, with whom, and for approximately how long will help to keep major problems from developing. Try to know at all times where your children are. Even if they move from one neighbor's home to another, it should be their responsibility to call you.

One of Lorna's standards is that the dinner hour—four times a week—is sacred, no matter what else is going on with the family. We have asked her kids what they think about the enforced dinner hour. All three of them say, "We like it. It keeps us close. We can support and encourage each other."

Encourage Your Children to Be Involved in Positive Activities

This may sound a little old-fashioned, but we believe at-risk kids have too much free time. Positive involvements often keep kids from getting into trouble. Kids least likely to get into trouble spend one or more hours a week in sports, clubs, music, drama, or other positive extracurricular activities.

To put it another way, bored kids eventually find trouble. Jim and Cathy suggest that you help your children find healthy activities that build confidence and self-esteem. For instance, they allow their children to choose their extracurricular activities. It's not a matter of if they are involved; it's a matter of which activities they choose. Christy likes ballet and baseball (what a combo)! Rebecca shifted to gymnastics after she realized ballet wasn't for her. The littlest, Heidi, wants to do it all but is permitted to choose only one or two activities at a time. Their rules are minimal but important. Our children don't have to excel but must try to do their best. Games, practices, and rehearsals are mandatory during the season of each activity. Consider giving this system a try. It will help keep your kids focusing on positive and fun learning experiences, and it'll give you more chances to cheer for your children.

Encourage Positive Peer Influence

People often discuss and write about the negative aspects of peer pressure rather than the positive value of healthy peer relationships. Peer influences may be the most profound influences in adolescents' lives. Kids today live in what sociologists call "friendship clusters" consisting of two to eight close friends. This means that instead of popularity and acceptance from the entire student body, kids basically need to gain a sense of belonging from their friendship clusters. Usually kids imitate their friendship clusters. When it comes to at-risk behavior or preventing risky behavior, parents can often determine which direction the stress is headed by simply knowing who their children's friends are.

If a teenager has two or three best friends who are experimenting with drugs, the odds are very good that he or she will also experiment with drugs. If a teenager's friends enjoy the music of Christian artist Amy Grant, the odds are favorable that he or she also enjoys Amy Grant's music. We tell students all the time, "You become like your friends. They have a profound influence on who you are and who you are becoming."

A Gallup survey concurs with that statement. In 1991, researchers asked teenagers, "What influences teenagers most?" Among the top five vote-getters were: friends, 87 percent; home, 51 percent; school, 45 percent; music, 41 percent; and television, 32 percent. Religion received a petty 13 percent of the vote; magazines and books ranked even lower.

However, our point is that peer influence is perhaps the most influential factor in adolescents' lives.

What's the implication for you as a parent? Monitor your children's friendships. Really get acquainted with your children and spend time with them. Consider making your home "Grand Central" to your children's friends. Personally, both of us and our wives would rather sacrifice a bit of household perfection and pay a little more for food in order to get to know our children's friends. Because their friends are so important, we choose to invite them for dinner or special evenings out. Positive friendships can prevent risky behavior.

Promote Sexual, Drug, and Alcohol Restraint

We don't want to oversimplify an important issue, but we must emphasize that kids who postpone sexual activity and choose not to get high on drugs or alcohol have a much better chance of reducing risky behavior.

Jim was on a talk show recently where the secular host quoted the statistic that at least 60 percent of kids have had sexual intercourse by age 19. "Everybody's doing it," the host said, expecting Jim to challenge the statistic. He didn't. He simply stated his opinion: "That means that 40 percent of the kids *aren't* doing it."

The host went on to quote from our book *Drug-Proof Your Kids* where we state that 87 percent of American kids will try alcohol by age 18. Again he said, "Everybody's doing it."

Jim responded, "It may be true that most kids experiment with alcohol and even a majority by age 18 will try an illicit drug, but our experience is that many wise young people are choosing to say no." The longer a person chooses to say no to drugs, alcohol, and sex, the more the risk factors are reduced.

Does this mean you should place your kids in a closet or move to the desert until they turn 18? No (although at times you may think about it!). It does mean that you can't afford not to give your children proper sex and drug education, beginning at an early age. (We strongly urge you to read chapters five and six on sexuality and drug use, even if your children are very young.)

Promote a Positive School Environment

Your kids will spend more waking hours involved in school activities than any other activities. So it's not surprising that when asked about stress in their lives, kids usually list school as number one or two. Teenagers who don't exhibit at-risk behavior are twice as likely as other kids to be involved in a positive school environment. Kids who continue their education by going to college or trade school after graduating from high school are most likely to thrive in later life.

As a parent, you must do everything you can to help provide your children with a positive school experience. This means work—at least helping your children "win" at school. Usually this means monitoring homework and classroom activity. It also means taking an active interest in their world—much of which revolves around school. A busy dad in our neighborhood, for example, volunteers in his son's class once a week, and his son really appreciates his father's experiencing his "turf."

If you have concerns about your child's school, you can make a difference. Jim's wife, Cathy, for example, heard that their school district was considering a humanistic, ungodly, and downright gross literature curriculum. She obtained samples of the curriculum and distributed them to neighbors and friends, who were grateful for the information and joined her in the fight for a better literature program. The school board meeting at which the decision to accept the curriculum was to be made had the largest attendance ever; and the school board members, who had been unanimously in favor of the project, ended up rejecting it because of the community's input.

It may be necessary to sacrifice other aspects of your budget to enroll your children in a private Christian school. Cathy and Jim have recently done this, and their kids are thriving in this new environment. No matter which decision you make about sending your children to public or private schools, do whatever you can to make school a positive environment. The results are worth the time and effort.

Help to Foster a Spiritual Life

Church involvement and the development of an inner spiritual life cannot be overlooked as major factors in preventing risky behavior. Although all the crisis issues discussed in this book are found within the lives of church members, the risk factors will be reduced as you and your children cultivate more church involvement and attention to your relationship with God. Studies show that young people who pray and read Scripture daily reduce their risk of drug abuse by half. As we come in contact with committed Christian young people all over the world, we get to know kids who have the strength to say no to risky behavior.

Troy, for example, is from a divorced home. He was abused as a child. His grades were poor. When he was in tenth grade, a friend brought him to our youth group. He had no religious background but viewed the youth group as a fun, positive, uplifting place to be. During the winter snow camp, he made a commitment to Jesus Christ. Did all his problems go away? No. In fact, some family issues intensified. Yet through his relationship with Christ, positive adult role models in the youth group, and a healthy peer environment, Troy didn't choose to go the route of the majority of kids from negative backgrounds. Christ made the difference in his life. He can make a difference in your children's lives as well.

There's no vaccine that inoculates kids against the problems discussed in this book. There are no easy answers that shelter young people from the onslaught of personal disruption and the longtime scars of negative environments and behaviors. However, we believe that if you adopt the right attitude and are willing to work hard at preventing risky behavior, positive results will be evident in your children's lives.

CHAPTER FIVE

Sex

Recently, Jim spoke at a large high school in central California on the subject of sex and dating. In a school poll taken before he spoke in favor of abstaining from sexual intercourse until marriage, the kids were asked to choose one of the following:

1. I will choose to have sexual intercourse before marriage.
2. I will choose to not have sexual intercourse before marriage.
3. I am undecided.

When school counselors tallied up the results, 68 percent of the student body were undecided! After Jim's presentation, only 24 percent were undecided. The vast majority chose abstinence. They made a commitment to wait until marriage. Many kids don't take the "sexual-purity challenge" simply because it's not offered to them. Let's look at what one husband and wife are doing in this area.

The Sexual-Purity Challenge

As busy parents, John and Carolyn do a marvelous job when it comes to helping their three beautiful daughters deal with one of the most dominant issues of life: SEX. Along with several thousand other concerned parents, John and Carolyn are offering the "sexual-purity challenge."

Between the ages of 10 and 13, each daughter has accompanied her parents on a special weekend outing. Each one picked the place to stay (within financial reason) and whatever fun experience she wanted. Tawnie chose a play in Los Angeles. Stephanie wanted to hang out at the beach. The youngest, Amber, chose a Los Angeles Lakers basketball game. How's that for diversity!

During each special outing, John, Carolyn, and one of the girls played hard and ate fun food. The theme of each weekend was the sexual-purity challenge. They talked a lot about the birds and the bees. They listened to a tape together and read a chapter from Jim's book *Radical Respect*. Each daughter was different. The two more outgoing girls talked and talked, asking questions that made John and Carolyn blush a little. The quietest child listened, took it all in, had a great time, but didn't say much.

On Sunday, before they returned home, John and Carolyn asked each daughter, "Are you willing to say to God, 'I commit my sexuality to you and will refrain from sexual intercourse until marriage'?" Each girl said yes without pressure, and the parents gave each daughter a little necklace as a reminder of taking the sexual-purity challenge.[1]

Let's be honest. Will every kid who made a decision at school or with parents to remain abstinent until marriage actually do so? No. Depending on which poll you look at, at least 50 percent of the teenagers in the United States have already had sexual intercourse by age 18. But "everybody" isn't doing it. We parents need to help our kids make the right and wise decision to refrain, and our efforts will make an impact.

A couple who attended Jim's youth group decided years later to get married. Jim had the privilege of doing their premarital counseling and performing the wedding. During the counseling, he always has a session on sex. Frankly, couples usually squirm a bit in that session. In today's world, most people who enter a marital relationship after age 18 aren't virgins—including Christians.

Derrick started the session by saying, "I know we are going to talk about sex today, and we wanted to tell you a story." Immediately Jim got ready for a negative one. But to his surprise, it was quite positive. Derrick continued:

> When Jennifer was in tenth grade, she sat in a Sunday school class you were teaching, and you asked the group to make a commitment to

remain sexually pure. She made that commitment and kept it. At camp a few years before that, you were giving your "sex talk" and asked us to wait until marriage. At that camp, I made a commitment to do just that. Just yesterday, Jennifer and I were talking about the fact that we are the only virgins we know and how even for us it hasn't been easy. I asked her what kept her from "going all the way." She told me her Sunday school story. I told her my camp story. We sit here today to tell you this stuff works!

Jim's response? Not surprisingly, he got choked up. Jim speaks to more than one hundred thousand students a year about sex, and he still finds the latest statistics hard to believe.

- Twelve million teens are sexually active. Eight out of 10 males and seven out of 10 females report having had intercourse while teenagers.
- If present trends continue, 40 percent of today's 14-year-old girls will be pregnant at least once before age 20.
- By age 20, 81 percent of today's unmarried males and 67 percent of today's unmarried females have had sexual intercourse.
- Fifty percent of all sexually active 19-year-old males had their first sexual experience between the ages of 11 and 13. Among nonvirgins, 50 percent of the boys and 18 percent of the girls first had intercourse at age 18 or younger.

- Seventy-four percent of teenagers say that they would live with someone before marriage or instead of getting married.
- More than 500,000 babies are born each year to unmarried American girls under age 18. Furthermore, about 80 percent of these teenage mothers are from low-income families.
- Teenage mothers cost taxpayers about $16 billion a year in welfare benefits alone. (The cost in dollars is only a minor aspect of what happens in the lives of pregnant teenagers and teenage married couples. The emotional and spiritual damage done to sexually promiscuous young people creates even greater damage.)[2]

Contrary to what many kids learn today, there's no such thing as "safe sex." The safe-sex movement in our world has relegated sex to an action without taking into consideration the emotional, psychological, and spiritual issues. The sexual-revolution crisis is perceived quite differently today, depending on people's perspectives. The popular, secular view is that the crisis is the "result" of promiscuity: AIDS, venereal disease, and unwanted pregnancies. However, the Christian perspective is concerned with the development of healthy morals and values—right and wrong—and deals with the issues of sin and obedience to God. The Christian view of sex takes into consideration a responsibility for one's actions and people's relationship with God.

Unfortunately, most young people receive their

sex education from the media. As mentioned previously, the average high school student had the opportunity to watch 14,000 acts of intercourse or innuendo to intercourse on prime-time TV in 1991, and he or she will watch an average of 10 hours a week of MTV this year. Kids today are fooled into "instant intimacy" because of such blatantly promiscuous sex. Television, movies, and much of rock music glorify sex and fill kids' senses with activities, images, and remarks about sexual activity while downplaying the responsibility that sexual activity requires.

However, even more unfortunate than the media's treatment of sex is the fact that only about 10 percent of children today receive positive, Christian sex education. Did you? Probably not. Even with the outstanding material on sexuality available to families and churches today, it's sad to say that we, as Christian parents, have done a poor job overall of helping our young people deal with this dominant issue. Sexuality isn't an easy subject to discuss with our kids, but it's unfortunate that so many parents and churches have remained more or less silent.

Our silence is really hurting this generation of young people who desire to hear the truth. Many kids have learned myths rather than facts about sex and its powerful consequences. An entire generation of young people has been left to experiment and learn about sex on its own. The lack of positive moral standards and basic understanding about sex often leads young people to participate in premature sexual activity.

You Can Make a Difference

We believe that most parents really desire to talk with their kids about sex. Unfortunately, most parents didn't receive positive, healthy sex education when they were growing up, so they have few or no role models to guide them in helping their children. If you're one of the vast majority of parents who care deeply about their children and yet aren't exactly sure what to say about sexuality or how to bring up the subject, don't be alarmed. Here are a few suggestions:

Be Willing to Talk About Sexuality

Kids need adults—especially parents—who will talk openly and honestly about sexuality and will listen. By doing so, you may prevent your kids from having some very negative experiences. You will also be giving them the gift of a healthy attitude toward sexuality and encouraging them to use one of God's most special gifts to us as He intended.

Parents always ask us, "What do we say to our children, and at what age?" To answer that question, we want to tell a joke.

One afternoon, seven-year-old Johnny came home from school, walked into the kitchen, and asked his mother, "Hey, Mom, what's sex?" Her face turned bright red, but not wanting to appear too shocked by the question she fumbled for the right words to say. *Where's my husband when I need him?* she thought. *This question was supposed to come about six years from now!*

Composing herself, she asked Johnny to sit at the kitchen table, poured him a glass of milk, and placed a plate of cookies in front of him that he happily received. She then proceeded to explain every detail of the birds and the bees to Johnny for the next 45 minutes. Johnny didn't say a word; he just ate those cookies! When she finished telling Johnny basically everything she knew about sex in explicit detail, Mom took a deep breath and said, "Well, Johnny, do you have any questions?"

He looked up, puzzled, and said, "Yeah, just one. How am I supposed to put all that on this soccer application where it says: Sex, M or F, please circle?"

Of course, Johnny's mother misread his question, but her situation illustrates a key point. As parents, we need to discuss sex in a positive, healthy way with our kids. However, sex education must be age appropriate. Our secular media and even our public school system have given kids too much too soon. It's like feeding a piece of steak to a baby who has no teeth. The baby chokes. But the opposite extreme is also dangerous. Some parents wait until it's too late. Let's quickly review a few more facts.

More than half of the high schoolers in the United States have had sex, according to a Centers for Disease Control survey. The following breakdown by grade reveals how high the percentages are:

- 9th grade — 40 percent
- 10th grade — 48 percent

- 11th grade — 57 percent
- 12th grade — 72 percent [3]

When Jim speaks to junior high and high school students about sex, he encourages them to write out questions. Here's a sample of the questions asked recently at a "Handling Your Hormones" youth event that more than 800 kids attended at Chuck Swindoll's former church in Fullerton, California. (Most of the kids were Christians.)

- How far is too far?
- Is it possible to get the pill without your parents knowing?
- How often do married people usually have sexual intercourse?
- Is oral sex okay?
- How do girls masturbate?
- How do boys masturbate?
- At what age do boys have their first erection?
- When is a girl's most dangerous time of the month? Is the pill expensive? Is the pill dangerous?
- What types of VD are there?
- I'm afraid of AIDS. What can I do to not get it?
- If you participate in oral sex, are you still a virgin?
- Will God condemn you if you have premarital sex? Will He forgive you?
- What can a guy do if he has a problem of lust toward other guys? How can you handle it without having to be gay?

- Does God forgive Christians who have had abortions?
- After someone has been sexually abused for years and hasn't told anyone about it, how can someone try to forget and deal with it?

As you can see, kids aren't just interested in the biological aspects of their sexuality. These types of questions are always asked. Interestingly, in recent years, kids are asking more and more questions about sexual abuse, homosexuality, pornography, oral sex, abortion, and birth control.

Teach Biblical Sexuality

We believe that today's generation of kids actually desires morals and values. Growing up in a basically value-neutral society hasn't given kids a healthy sexual foundation. A 17-year-old woman recently told Jim, "This is the first time in my life I've ever heard that God wants me to abstain from intercourse until marriage. Now that I think about it, it makes a lot of sense."

It's important for kids today to realize that the Bible speaks to important issues of the day. God created sex, and He views His creation as being very good. He wants the best for His children; that's why He places limits on premarital sexual activity.

Here are six Scripture passages that directly speak to our children (and us parents) about sexuality. We took this from an excellent article in *Discipleship Journal* by John Nieder:[4]

Genesis 1:27-28 and 2:18-25:

1. God created two distinct sexes.
2. God told the man and the woman to have children.
3. The man was created incomplete and in need of a helper.
4. No other creature could meet the man's need.
5. God made a woman to meet the man's need (and vice versa).
6. The man and the woman were supposed to join their lives and their bodies for life.
7. The sexual relationship was commanded before sin entered human experience.

2 Samuel 13:1-20:

1. Inappropriate sexual desire can lead to sin.
2. Wrong friends encourage wrong behavior.
3. Sexual sin often involves deception.
4. We should avoid potentially compromising situations.
5. Intense sexual desires can cause irrational actions.
6. When lust is fulfilled and desires diminish, the ensuing guilt may result in hatred.
7. Once the immoral act has occurred, irreparable damage has been done.
8. Alienation, hatred, and even violence can result from sexual sin.

Proverbs 5:

1. Children should follow their parents' wisdom.
2. We should watch out for and avoid sexual

temptations and sensuous allurements.

3. Sexual sins have terrible consequences.
4. We should flee temptation.
5. Sexual immorality can lead to disease.
6. Sexual intercourse should occur only in marriage.
7. Marital love is to be enjoyed.
8. God watches everything we do, including our sexual activity.

1 Corinthians 6:9-20:

1. Sexual sins can be forgiven.
2. Our bodies are devoted to God, not to sexual immorality.
3. Our bodies are important enough to be resurrected.
4. We should flee, not fight, temptation.
5. Sexual sin hurts us and can harm our bodies.
6. God owns us.
7. Jesus died to purchase us, so we should honor Him with our bodies.

1 Corinthians 7:1-9:

1. Unmarried people have a greater freedom to serve God.
2. Sex outside of marriage is always wrong.
3. The solution for passion is a marriage partner, not a boyfriend or a girlfriend.
4. God wants married couples to have free access to each others' bodies.
5. Men and women, husbands and wives, have strong sexual desires.

6. A couple's spiritual union should be more important than their physical union.
7. Free access to one's spouse reduces sexual temptation.

1 Thessalonians 4:1-8:

1. Living a pure life pleases God.
2. God's will is that we avoid sexual immorality.
3. God wants us to learn how to control our bodies.
4. Our methods of controlling our desires must be holy and honorable.
5. The way we control our bodies will differ from the methods of unbelievers.
6. Gratifying our sexual desires outside of marriage offends and detracts from the other person.
7. We shouldn't take advantage of another person in order to satisfy our sexual desires.
8. These standards come from God, not from man.
9. If we disobey these instructions, we reject God.

The Bible isn't a sex manual, yet it's very clear on certain sexual issues. Far too many kids today believe that God is the great killjoy when it comes to sex because they honestly don't know what the Bible says about it. A whole group of kids today has heard only what appear to be negative verses or unreal expectations when biblical sexuality has been discussed.

As parents, we must present biblical sexuality positively. God created sex. In the confines of marriage, it is wonderful. He put sexual boundaries in the Bible because He loves us and wants the best for us. Far too many young people are moving into marriage with a great deal of sexual-related baggage from previous relationships. God knows how devastating that baggage can be.

Following are questions we ask young people who have been having sexual intercourse or who are close to compromising their virginity. We're convinced that any couple contemplating premarital intercourse should look at and deal with these questions honestly.[5]

1. Will premarital intercourse lessen the meaning of intercourse in marriage for either of you? (Notice that in all these questions, both people are included in the decision-making process.)

2. Does your conscience make you feel uneasy during or after sexual intercourse? Could this be the Holy Spirit challenging you?

3. Are you both equally committed to each other?

4. Are you totally convinced in your hearts that the other person is "the one" forever?

5. What do you believe the Bible has to say about premarital sexual intercourse? Here are a few verses to look at: 1 Thessalonians 4:1-8; 1 Peter 2:11; 1 Corinthians 6:13, 18-20; Ephesians 5:3; and Acts 15:20.

6. You both seem to desire God's best for you. Will having sexual intercourse affect your usefulness to God or your relationship with Him?

7. Will having sexual intercourse before marriage damage in any way your relationship with each other?

8. Could premarital intercourse damage your communication or result in either a loss of respect for or mistrust of each other?

9. Will premarital intercourse help, hinder, or not affect your spiritual relationship with each other?

10. Have you thought through the possibilities of parenthood and marriage because of pregnancy?

11. What are your motives for having sexual intercourse? Are they pure?

Find Positive, Healthy Resources to Share with Kids

There are many excellent resources available for kids and parents on this subject. Use the gifts and abilities of others to help your child receive appropriate sex education.

We know there's hope. As parents, we can make a difference! Please don't leave all the responsibility of sex education and prevention of pregnancy to people who care less about your kids than you do. Listen to the words of Alice, age 18:

I really believe I'll be a virgin on the day of my wedding. My parents were always open about sex with me. They challenged me to give my body to God. I've done that. It's not always easy, but my commitment is strong, thanks to the input I received from my folks.

CHAPTER SIX

Substance Abuse

One Friday, we traveled to Philadelphia to conduct a three-hour "Drug-Proof Your Kids" seminar at a local school. During the flight, we picked up a copy of *USA Today* and noticed that cities were listed in order of the greatest number of people arrested who had illegal drugs in their systems. Philadelphia was at the top of the list. The writer was making the point that Philadelphia had the worst drug problem in the nation. So we felt great about doing our seminar. We knew we had some answers for people who badly needed them.

With great anticipation, we arrived at the auditorium. The program was scheduled to start at 7:00 P.M., but by 7:30 no one had come. So we packed up our outlines and went to dinner. This was one more glaring example of how easy it is for parents to avoid facing one of the worst temptations almost every child faces every day. Many parents deny that drug use, abuse, and addiction are problems in their homes. When minor symptoms of drug abuse develop, these same parents may pray that the symptoms will go away rather than taking constructive, preventive action. As a result, minor problems often escalate into major ones.

Our hope is that you will read this chapter and be motivated to do something to stop our nation's drug epidemic. There's plenty to be done; it just takes people who care enough to act.

As we begin to give you solutions to substance abuse, we want to present three cases, the most extreme one from Philadelphia first.

Nathan's father (long gone from the family) was an alcoholic. Kevin, Nathan's older brother, had been dealing drugs since he was in the eighth grade. His mother started using prescription tranquilizers soon after her husband's departure, while she was pregnant with her third child. Although she kept a fairly clean house, cooked dinners, and provided clothes for the kids, she was emotionally indifferent to her two boys and little girl, who was nearly six years younger than Nathan.

Nathan's maternal grandparents lived in the same urban area of Philadelphia and were nominal church-goers. They cared for and protected his younger sister, Rachel, because she was the only girl and the youngest child. Perhaps, too, they realized that their daughter was not giving Rachel sufficient attention.

However, they considered the boys old enough to take care of themselves.

Alone and ignored, Nathan found a peer group with whom he felt something in common. He began smoking marijuana at the end of the sixth grade with two other "misfits," mostly for camaraderie. He identified with his two friends, who also came from broken homes and were independent of any strong adult supervision. He felt that smoking a little marijuana was harmless fun and that it created a "family" bond between the three.

In ninth grade, Nathan moved up to beer and hard liquor, this time to escape the pain of living in poverty with too much pressure and too little future. The alcohol also took the edge off his pain of feeling unwanted and unloved. He didn't even need the social circle of his friends to drink; he went off on his own to seek "liquid comfort." During the next several years, he used whatever substances were available to ease his pain. By the end of high school, he was abusing any drug he could get his hands on. Nathan's story is typical of how the drug war is being lost in the inner city, one child at a time.

Terry grew up in Rancho Palos Verdes, a wealthy Los Angeles suburb filled with expensive homes, pristine schools, and overflowing churches. He came from an exemplary Christian family. His father had a good career. His mother devoted time to the community as a volunteer and to her family as a model wife and mother. He was clean-cut, a star athlete, an excellent student with a B+ average, and an active participant in church activities.

During summer camp his sophomore year, Terry became exposed to substance abuse. Older boys had smuggled beer, wine, and marijuana into the camp. That week, Terry tried all three. Although he didn't care that much for the taste of alcohol and wasn't crazy about smoking, he enjoyed the peer approval, the respect of the older guys, and especially the slight high he got from the drugs.

Instead of gaining a thirst for the outdoors, Terry returned home with a thirst for a regular high. His experimentation opened up a whole new world of friends and experiences in marijuana and alcohol. He relished the idea of having the approval of the fast crowd while maintaining his reputation as a Christian leader in his student group at church.

"Sure, I felt guilty," Terry said later. "I knew my parents would just die if they ever found out. They are fairly knowledgeable. They don't even drink champagne. I knew if I could keep a fairly clean, 'straight' appearance, they'd never suspect anything."

Eventually, Terry was not able to maintain his "straight" appearance. Regular bouts with drinking and drugs led to the inevitable—a need for a higher high—and be became hooked on cocaine. His ability to concentrate slipped, as did his grades, friendships, girlfriends, and home life. As Terry recalled later, "I became a slave to cocaine."

Karalynn, a high school junior, came from a solid,

middle-class family. Her father had begun recovering from alcoholism two years earlier, but his mood swings, especially the mean temper that had come out during his heavy drinking spells, were still fresh in Karalynn's mind. "I'll never be like that," Karalynn promised herself and her close friends. She abhorred her father's personality changes, his helpless enslavement to hard liquor, and the embarrassment of his slurred speech and drunken behavior.

Karalynn became involved with high school drama productions in ninth grade. After each performance, the "theater gang" held parties at various students' houses. With or without parental approval or knowledge, kids brought along alcohol. Karalynn always drank to be part of the gang, but she was proud of the fact that she never got drunk. My determination and willpower, she told herself, will never allow me to get drunk or be an alcoholic like my dad.

Even the upper-class boys were impressed that Karalynn could out-drink them when she was still only a freshman—and barely show any signs of wear. While her girlfriends were getting sleepy after two or three beers, other students were dizzily staggering through the house, and even one or two of the heavy-drinking boys were getting ill, Karalynn would be calmly drinking her sixth beer and showing none of their symptoms. In fact, kids often nominated her to be the "designated driver" for the gang because she was never drunk.

No one understood at the time that Karalynn was well on her way to becoming an alcoholic.

Those stories are similar to hundreds of others with which we are familiar. They illustrate that alcoholism and drug addiction are no respecters of persons—whether rich or poor, black or white, Christian or unchurched. The mechanism for addiction, the attraction of illicit substances, and the progression of substance abuse develop along similar and predictable lines.

More than three million teenagers in the United States are chemically dependent on marijuana, alcohol, speed, crack, LSD, PCP, heroin, cocaine, barbiturates, inhalants, narcotics, stimulants, and/or a variety of designer drugs. By the time a child has finished high school, the chances are:

- 85 percent of experimenting with alcohol.
- 57 percent of trying an illegal drug.
- 33 percent of smoking marijuana on some occasion.
- 25 percent of smoking marijuana regularly.
- 17 percent of trying cocaine or crack.[1]

Those are conservative estimates, but they should come as no surprise.

It's startling just how bad substance abuse has become in America. Our nation has 5 percent of the world's population, yet it uses 50 percent of the world's cocaine. Our streets have become so drug saturated that the drug cartels are trying to expand into the developing countries of Europe. At every level, it appears that America has lost this war, and many parents have stopped fighting. Let's look at several commonly abused substances and their effects on kids, families, and the United States as a whole.

Tobacco: Gateway to Marijuana

Cigarette use may be down among adults, but it's way up among youth. And no wonder. Recently, a group of elementary school kids were shown a picture of the Camel cigarettes' mascot. As many kids were able to name this cartoon character as could name Mickey Mouse. If something related to smoking is so familiar to children, it shouldn't be surprising that so many adolescents take up the habit. Role models at home are definitely at play here also: 75 percent of the kids who smoke have parents who smoke.

By now, everyone knows plenty about the dangers of tobacco. It kills more than 52,000 Americans each year through chronic lung disease. But more important, it is now understood that tobacco is a "gateway" to illicit drug use. For instance, 80 percent of the kids who smoke tobacco will try marijuana, compared to only 21 percent of nonsmokers. Former White House drug chief Robert DuPont compiled even more frightening statistics about cigarette-smoking 12- to 17-year-olds. This group of young smokers is:

- 2 times as likely as nonsmokers to use alcohol.
- 9 times as likely to ingest depressants and stimulants.
- 10 times as likely to smoke marijuana.
- 14 times as likely to use cocaine, hallucinogens, and heroin.

Marijuana

Every day, Americans smoke 85,000 pounds of marijuana. This marijuana is now 5 to 20 times stronger than it was 10 years ago. Its long-ranging effects, its potency, and its dangers far exceed the "dope" that people considered harmless during the '60s.[2]

When a midwestern school district polled parents about the drug situation, more than 80 percent of them agreed that marijuana was a major problem for seventh through twelfth graders. Yet only 20 percent thought their children were actually involved. The reality? More than half of the student body had tried marijuana and nearly one-third admitted smoking marijuana regularly.[3]

Cocaine and Crack Cocaine

Cocaine—also known as coke, rock, freebase, snow, "doing a line," crack, crank, flake, snow, blow, and "C"—is one of the most serious and terrifying drugs for young people today. It's serious because in its most widespread form, crack, it has become the "in" drug among middle-class and upper-middle-class kids. In fact, while many inner-city kids are strung out on crack, 75 percent of cocaine users are white kids from the suburbs, dispelling the idea that drugs are only a problem for poor, black, ghetto youth.

Crack is cheap (in most places, a vial of crack costs as little as $15) and readily available, making it extremely accessible to young people. Currently, 8 percent of high school students and 10 percent of college-age youth are regular users, and 1.3 percent of all sixth graders have tried it. A Colorado State University study of 1,472 seniors in 124 rural schools in seven states found crack in every school except one.[4]

Cocaine in any form is terrifying because it's the most highly addictive drug known. When the extreme euphoria wears off, the user is depressed—even suicidal—and has an intense physiological and psychological need to get the same high again. Numerous stories have been told about narcotics agents—FBI agents or city police—who have had to use cocaine when they're with suspected dealers so they won't expose their undercover status. Unfortunately, as a result of just one or two "snort sessions," some law-enforcement personnel have developed an intense craving for the very drug they are trying to wipe out.

Cocaine is also unpredictable and can kill during a person's first use. There's no way to control dosages, to know potency, or to know which powders have been used to "cut" the cocaine. Heart angina, palpitations, arrhythmia, and death can occur when cocaine disrupts the brain's control of the heart and respiration—even the first time a person tries the drug. In 1991, emergency rooms treated 46,202 cases of cocaine use, up from 8,000 the previous year.

More than 21 million people in the United States have tried cocaine, and 2.4 million use it occasionally. Currently, there are one million cocaine addicts in the

United States, and every day, approximately five thousand people—teenagers and adults who should know better—try cocaine for the first time.[5]

Alcohol: The Drug of Choice

Alcohol is a drug. We are continually amazed to hear parents say, "At least my kids are using only alcohol. I'm glad they're not on drugs." Alcohol, although legally and socially acceptable for adults, is a drug. *Its use is against the law for children.*

So it is illegal—and wrong—for kids to drink socially. Laws against minors drinking have been instituted for good reasons. Their young bodies are not as capable of handling alcohol as adult bodies, and young people are not at a stage where they can drink responsibly. There are not many adults, either, who can be labeled as "responsible" drinkers. Alcohol-related highway accidents are the number-one killer of 15- to 24-year-olds.[6]

In a nationwide survey, *Newsweek* magazine found that 66 percent of high school students in America believe that alcohol and other drugs are the biggest problems facing them. No wonder. Their first drinking experience now occurs around age 12. It's no longer unusual to find 10- or 12-year-olds who have serious drinking problems.[7]

During the last 25 years, the number of high school students who become intoxicated at least once a month has doubled. Some schools report that as many as 11 percent of their students are alcoholics.

Research conducted by *U.S. News and World*

Report found that two out of every three high school seniors had consumed alcohol within the previous month and that 5 percent of high school seniors drink daily.[8]

A terrible trend has surfaced within the past several years. Kids are giving up other drugs and using alcohol in large quantities to produce extreme intoxication. In a way similar to a person mainlining drugs, they use funnels to ingest as much alcohol as they can as fast as they can. One person holds the funnel while the other person pours the booze down the throat. Then they wait to see the effect. As a result of this type of drinking, emergency room personnel are treating more alcohol overdoses than ever before. People used to think it wasn't possible to drink enough alcohol to kill oneself. Methods today's kids have developed are making it happen.

Peer pressure to drink is a powerful force that overcomes thousands of kids every day. But peer pressure isn't the only one kids have to counter. The other big pressure comes from media advertising. The liquor industry, which pays many millions of dollars to advertise to an ever-younger drinking generation, has a well-developed plan to convert nondrinkers into regular drinkers. The strategy of the brewing companies and liquor industry, as reported in *The Bottom Line on Alcohol in Society,* is to:

- increase the number of occasions in which alcohol will be appropriately consumed.
- increase the percentage of those who drink.

Witness their outreach into the college market and popularizing the "Spuds MacKenzie" and "Red Dog" party-dog image for beer-drinking students (many of whom are underage).

- position alcohol as "thirst quenchers" and "refreshment beverages" to compete directly with soft drinks. (Witness the development of wine coolers or even the Jack Daniels' ads for "Lynchburg Lemonade.")
- position alcohol as part of a healthy, clean-living lifestyle. (Witness the brewing industry's sponsorship of major sporting events.) [9]

Clearly, that marketing strategy is paying off. In just six years, there has been a 150 percent increase among sixth graders sampling alcohol, 40 percent of whom have already tasted wine coolers.[10]

Why Kids Use Drugs

In helping parents counter drug use in their homes, we have tried to help them understand why children are attracted to something so dangerous. In "the old days," it was curiosity. That motivation seems to fade further away each year. The new motivations are:

Peer Approval and Acceptance

These are extremely important to kids at the junior high through high school levels. Peer pressure is without a doubt one of the most compelling reasons a kid will try drugs. The concept of "just say no," while valid, is useless when kids don't want to say no. They very much want to say yes when they are likely to win approval and acceptance from their crowd. The idea of being different or standing out from the crowd is difficult for kids. About the only way they can endure it is when family values outweigh the need for peer acceptance. In other words, kids who say no almost always feel tremendous love and acceptance in their strong families. Rarely does a child from such a family rebel against a rule or a regulation. When a child from such a family does rebel, he rebels against the relationship. You can see that the relationship with the parent is the biggest defense that parent has against peer pressure.

Experimentation

Some drug use is actually experimentation. There's a curiosity: "I wonder what it's really like." This is why it's so important for parents to be informed and to tell kids the truth about drugs. Kids will quickly disregard scare stories that aren't based on fact.

As one student put it, "I kept hearing all this bull—from my parents on how marijuana would make you hallucinate and go crazy and that you would look like a bum if you were on it. But the whole time they were telling me this, my best friend and another buddy were getting high almost every weekend, and I could see that none of it was true. So I thought if it isn't hurting them, it won't hurt me. I wanted to try to get high, too." Parents must have accurate information if they are to win the credibility battle with their kids.

Thrill and Attraction of the Forbidden

In the development of a child, there are two possible stages of rebellion and negativity: the "Terrible Twos" and the "Terrible Teens." During both periods, kids establish independence and experiment to find out where the boundaries lie. The thrilling lure of the forbidden is a strong one for teens who want to stand up to the yoke of parental authority, assert their individuality, and feel a sense of power over their lives.

My parents can't tell me what to do! they think. *I can decide on my own if I want to try this!* The thrill of acting grown-up and on their own, and denying their parents in the process, is part of the high. Again, the only counter to this is a strong relationship between parent and child.

Media Pressure

Pervasive pressure from the media sets up a false world for kids by continually telling them, "Everybody is doing it—and they're having a wonderful, glamorous time, too!" In a real sense, this is a subtle form of brainwashing that leaves children vulnerable to experimentation because it reinforces the idea that "everyone normal is doing this." Few role models or images presented by the media show that clean living is acceptable. Clean-living kids are usually set up to be squares, kooks, or in some way abnormal.

Rarely do the media present a sordid, unhappy picture of drug use. From television sitcoms to major motion pictures, alcohol is continually shown to be a part of a sophisticated and successful lifestyle. Almost any popular teen movie shows high school kids happily guzzling beer and wine. Never do we see the aftermath of a drunken teenage driver's mangled body being pulled from the wreck of a car. When the media portray the unhappy side of drug use, they inevitably show poor black people living in the ghetto rather than middle-class white kids in a nice neighborhood.

The Progression from Drug Use to Addiction

We wish that parents' good intentions alleviated all drug problems in their families. Of course, they don't. Adolescents continue to have free will and make destructive decisions, even if they are raised in healthy homes. The priority for parents is to act constructively as soon as possible when they see their children slipping or running into problems. Many parents we've talked to wish they had done more, sooner.

How adolescents' use and abuse of drugs turns into addiction isn't a mystery, because progression of drug use follows a fairly predictable pattern.

Experimentation

Whether from thrill-seeking motivation or peer pressure, most drug use starts on a trial basis. It is occasional, episodic, and usually done during the summer or on weekends with friends. Because of the adolescent's low tolerance, he or she easily feels buzzed or gets high.

Association with Regular Users

At this stage, the adolescent participates in regular weekend bashes where alcohol, pot, hash, or possibly pills are used. He or she stays out much later and is willing to suffer hangovers. This behavior is classified as abuse because it's illegal, immoral, and irresponsible. It's illegal because, obviously, it's against the law. It's immoral because drunkenness is clearly spoken against in the Bible. And it's irresponsible because the mixture of drugs, alcohol, and driving kills more teenagers than any other source of behavior.

Increased Abuse

This manifests itself when the adolescent is willing and wanting to get high alone, to use drugs during the week, or even to skip school to get high. Blackouts may begin. He or she holds conversations with friends about, "What did I do last night?"

Dependency

Increased abuse quickly progresses to the dependency stage, where the adolescent feels that he or she must have a drink or hit to make it through class, a test, or a weekend with Aunt Emily. Preoccupation with use begins. Being high becomes normal, and the source of supply becomes a worry. Straight friends are dropped, and drug dealing may begin.

Addiction

When the "I want to" have a drink or hit becomes "I must have," the adolescent has gone from having a problem to the problem having the adolescent. Now the use of the drug has precedence over anything and everything in life. The adolescent experiences a loss of control over drug use and becomes a slave to the drug.

Deterioration of Values

This follows closely after addiction. Stealing and lying become the norm. Trouble with the law—dealing, possession, and/or driving under the influence—enters in. Sexual involvement with other drug users and dealers most likely accompanies other delinquent behavior.

Personal and Family Crises

The adolescent's personal life is now out of control. Memory suffers; flashbacks—and also thoughts of suicide—may increase. The whole family feels out of control because one of its members isn't functioning. Although in a position of responsibility, parents are unable to change the adolescent's behavior—to stop the lying or abuse. Other siblings suffer because much of the conversation, concern, and time of the family are preoccupied with trying to restore the dysfunctional adolescent.

Feelings of Being Abandoned by God

In almost every case of addiction, the adolescent's relationship with God is severely damaged. The cheap substitute of a drug-induced stupor replaces spiritual experience. Separation from God turns into anger toward God. "How could You let this happen to me?" the adolescent may scream at God. "Why didn't You pull me out of this sooner?"

You Can Make a Difference

When a parent is ready to help a child, it's often out of desperation. At this point, there's often a senseless search for a "quick fix" or instant solution. The parent wants to change years of history in four weeks. Together, let's consider a comprehensive plan that parents can use at any point in the progression of substance abuse, especially before it starts.

Prevention Starts with You

Without a doubt, parents are the most effective weapons in the drug war. Parental attitude is the most important aspect of that weapon. Studies show that the best predictor of adolescents' drinking habits is the attitude and behavior of their parents toward alcohol. Generally, children are more prone to abuse drugs not only when their parents abuse drugs or alcohol, but also when their parents:

- smoke cigarettes.
- use any substance to help master stress.
- impart an ambivalent or even positive attitude toward drugs.[11]

Children are keenly aware when they observe their parents taking mood-altering drugs to alleviate distress or pain. A statement like "It has been a terrible day at the office, and I need a drink to unwind" speaks volumes to children and sets a precedent for their future behavior.

Parental attitude is important, but attitude can't alter genetic predisposition to addiction. Parents need to look carefully at their family histories to see if there's a predisposition to addiction among any blood relatives. If there is, the children need to be told about their genetic predisposition. Alcoholism runs in families, and its cause isn't something over which any family member can successfully exert power or mind control. Once the decision to drink is made, it is hard to overcome the genetic predisposition.

If there's an incident of alcoholism among your relatives, help your children understand that it would be wise for all relatives, even those of legal age, to abstain from alcohol. Explain that one sure sign of alcoholism is, in fact, a high tolerance for alcohol— the ability to "hold alcohol" or "drink someone under the table." Often adolescents believe the ability to hold a lot of alcohol is a virtue or sign of strength. All tolerance does, however, is allow people to consume enough of an addictive chemical to become addicted to it. If you have any indication that a child is drinking vast quantities of alcohol, most likely it's not use or experimentation; it's full-blown adolescent alcoholism.

The response of kids to information about genetic predisposition toward alcoholism has been fairly dramatic. When we present it during youth conferences, for instance, they immediately become angry and say things like, "It's not fair." Their reaction shows us that no one has taken the time to present the possibility of genetic predisposition to them. Their anger is, however, the first positive step that could lead them to turn away from drug use and abuse. So be sure to have an open and honest discussion of the family tree.

Education Starts with You

One of the most glaring truths we have discovered about parenthood is that a good parent is a good teacher. A good teacher is always searching for teachable moments. They come out of nowhere while watching television or eating ice cream after a movie. During such moments, drugs or drinking need to be addressed with children and adolescents. We hope you haven't relegated this type of education of your children to someone else and that you continually look for opportunities to teach your children the truth about alcohol and other drugs.

Parents should be prepared to speak about drug abuse by the time their children are in third grade. Regular heart-to-heart talks should not stop once the children are adolescents. At this point, such discussions may become more difficult, but they are also more essential to keep the lines of communication open. The education that begins early should continue as long as your children live under your roof.

When parents know and teach facts about alcohol and other drugs, they do more than just give their children a good drug-education course. In fact, the information itself may not always warn kids away. But the parents' willingness to teach and discuss and listen indicates to their children that they are in control of the situation, that they are informed, and that they know exactly what's going on. Knowing their parents are aware, knowledgeable, and prepared to deal with the issues speaks more to young people than stories about the dangers of drugs, no matter how valid such stories may be.

Scare tactics are rarely effective because adolescents have a difficult time comprehending that the dangers of drugs actually could affect them. Although adolescents may physically and intellectually be capable of handling most anything adults can, they still lack critical-thinking skills that enable them to understand causes and effects over time—that is, long-range planning and long-term consequences.

This kind of destructive thinking was evident after the death of basketball star Len Bias. When kids were asked if the tragedy happened because of the dangers of cocaine, their answers were surprising. They didn't feel his death was due as much to cocaine as it was to his stupidity as a user. "If he had been more careful, he wouldn't have died" was the common rationalization. Even the death of a hero isn't enough to break through kids' denial and lack of understanding and maturity.

Put more simply, most adolescents find it impossible to plan and prepare anything further ahead than the Friday night party. That's why it's almost useless to tell teenagers that suntanning can produce wrinkles and skin cancer or that poor marks in ninth grade affect their chances to enroll in their colleges of choice. It's also why it is difficult for teens to understand how drugs will affect them over time. They feel invincible, that "it'll never happen to me." They generally are capable of understanding only what's happening to them here and now.

Besides disseminating drug information, parents can also help educate their children by training them to make responsible decisions and recognize responsible behavior. Parents should allow their children to make decisions for themselves as soon as possible and whenever appropriate. When they are allowed to make appropriate decisions:

- they begin to develop self-esteem, believing they are intelligent, worthy, and capable of making decisions. Children who enter adolescence in this frame of mind are often among the few who can "just say no" to drugs and walk away.
- they learn independence in a healthy, nurturing setting (rather than trying to assert it later by experimenting with drugs behind their parents' backs).
- they learn to observe the outcome of good choices and the ramifications of poor choices. Thus, they are being trained in critical-thinking skills that help them consider and understand long-term consequences.

Beginning to educate a 16-year-old about drugs and alcohol is too late. Most likely the child already knows more about those substances than his or her parents. Education must start early and continue into the late teen years. Since kids deal with the temptation of drugs almost every day, you need to be talking about it with your kids. If alcohol and other drug use is an avoided subject, you'll find it difficult to develop an honest relationship with your children. It's important to be able to talk about all subjects that confront your children every day.

Identification of Symptoms/Danger Signs

Prevention and education never work 100 percent of the time. So the best preventers and educators must be prepared to identify problem-related symptoms. Parental denial is often phenomenal at this point. A mother attending one of our seminars had found little pieces of foil, a pipe, white powder, and some dried leaves in her child's room. "Could this indicate a problem?" she asked. "Should I talk to my son about it?" The fact that she asked us these questions indicated that she already knew a problem existed. She just wasn't able to accept the problem because her denial was so strong.

There's a big difference between parents who think their children have a drug problem and those who know their children actually do! Denial and even naïveté are common among parents of adolescents who have drug problems. Often such problems are left to develop on their own because parents believe their children are just "going through a stage."

Although rebellion, pursuit of independence, and the development of new friends and ideas can be normal teenage behavior, you should become concerned if your teenager exhibits symptoms such as those listed below. If all or many of these are present, take immediate action. In and of themselves, these subtle signs don't necessarily indicate a problem. However, in combination, they often point to drug use, abuse, and addiction:

- secrecy
- change in friends, especially toward "fast" or "worldly" kids
- change in dress and appearance, especially wearing long sleeves or otherwise heavy clothing during warm weather
- increased isolation
- change in activities and interests, particularly when they don't seem to be positive replacements
- drop in grades, especially when there's no logical reason
- getting fired from an after-school job
- changes in behavior around home
- staying out all night
- dropping out of sports participation
- possession of a bottle of eye drops (to counter bloodshot eyes)

Less subtle signs that should grab your attention include:

- extreme withdrawal from the family
- increase in mysterious phone calls that produce a frantic reaction
- smoking, especially if you have a nonsmoking household
- money problems
- extreme change in weight (gain or loss)
- appearance of strange, new friends who are older than your child
- listening to heavy-metal rock with pro-drug lyrics
- acting disconnected or spacey
- dilated pupils
- suspicious paraphernalia, such as lighters, clips, or small spoons
- long periods of time in the bathroom[12]

Some parents refuse to accept even more blatant indicators. If your child is picked up for drug possession, for example, don't fall into the trap of believing that it was a setup or that people are being unfair to your child. Recognize the reality of your child's behavior, and establish a plan to help him or her.

An Intervention

If your child does have a substance-abuse problem, admitting it is your first step. Once you have broken through the denial and seen the reality of the problem, it's time to take action. It's time to intervene.

Intervention has proved to be effective in changing a drug-dependent child's behavior and starting his or her healing process and road to recovery. Simply put, intervention is one or more counseling sessions specifically designed to help the child see the need for change. When it's time to intervene, it's best for you to not do it alone. A professional can provide the greatest potential for success.

There are several reasons the process of intervention is usually successful. First, an intervention is handled by a professional who can remain objective and is immune to family members' emotional manipulation and its accompanying behavior, such as threats and yelling.

Second, when family members begin the intervention process, they will be instructed in how to confront the young person without anger and blame. When condemnation—hostilities and placing blame—aren't present, he or she will be better able to hear the family's concerns.

Third, intervention leads to a controlled confrontation where the adolescent is offered alternatives. He or she can seek help or face such unpleasant consequences as lack of financial support or a place to live. If your child demands to continue using drugs, the only alternative may be to ask him or her to live somewhere else. This decision is never easy, and intervention usually doesn't reach this point. But you must be willing to take this extreme measure in order to help your child. Addiction is powerful. It has stolen the lives of millions of children. You must be willing to follow through if you expect to help produce needed changes in your child's life.

Treatment

If your child's problem is severe enough, it may be beyond the scope of weekly counseling sessions. It may be necessary to seek help through a treatment program. To ensure that your child will obtain quality treatment, however, you must evaluate several important factors before agreeing to place your child in a treatment program.

Quality treatment addresses the whole person—his or her physical, mental, emotional, social, and spiritual dimensions. The treatment program brings a variety of forces together in a controlled environment to initiate positive changes. Since the program is so powerful, it's vital that you find one that will stay true to your values. Many secular programs, for example, place no emphasis on Christ. There are a number of Christian treatment centers, so you'll be able to find help for your child that is consistent with your values.

Several different types or levels of treatment are listed below to help you make a wise decision for your child should circumstances dictate.

Inpatient Hospital

This treatment, conducted in a hospital, utilizes a full complement of doctors, nurses, and other professionals trained in social work, psychology, and counseling. It is the most comprehensive, keeps the patient in a protective environment, and is covered by most insurance plans.

Residential Treatment

Less expensive than hospital care, this treatment isn't always covered by insurance plans. Some people are too sick to enter this type of program because in order to keep costs down, there are fewer doctors and nurses on staff, and it is a less-protective environment.

Halfway House

This treatment provides a place of separation and a less-protective environment. All the patients in the house are recovering, and most of them attend school during the day and counseling sessions or Alcoholics or Narcotics Anonymous meetings at night.

Day Treatment

This includes everything provided by residential treatment except that all treatment takes place during the day and the patient returns home at night. This isn't a good choice when home separation is needed or when an addict in the initial stages of recovery can't control the urge to use. Day treatment is less expensive than inpatient care, but insurance coverage may not be available.

Outpatient Care

Occurring after school or work, this type of treatment works well for some patients. This program must be highly structured to be successful, especially with kids who are not yet committed to recovery. It works best for kids in the experimental stage of drug use who are not yet classified as addicts.

Wilderness Treatment

New Life Clinics provide Christ-centered treatment in the wilderness that lasts 52 days. Trained field staff, combined with licensed therapists, provide a unique experience for kids who need the added benefit of open space. Parents attend the last few days of the program when family issues are addressed. We wish we could tell you about other similar programs, but we don't know of any other programs like these where Christians counselors are teamed with qualified field staff. Parents of children involved in the program have been highly enthusiastic.

Components of Quality Care

Choosing a treatment resource is never easy. We recommend that you talk with at least two parents who have had kids in the program before making this important decision. In addition to counselors and therapists, other parents are often the best judge of the program's quality. When you research a program, be sure that all the indicators point toward a quality program. Indicators to look for include:

- a well-maintained facility
- a referral by someone you trust
- a referral by someone who has been through the program
- a strong team approach to treatment
- personal attention, including individual sessions
- treatment that also involves the patient's family

- sensitive and service-oriented staff members
- support of traditional values
- supervision of television, music, reading materials, dress, language, expressed attitudes, and visitors

Understanding God's Healing Power

We believe that God's power is vitally important in healing from addiction. So we can't overemphasize how crucial it is that you find a treatment program that is rooted in Scripture and the power of the living God. The first step in the process of healing from addiction is for the addict to acknowledge, "I can't handle this, but God can. I will let Him do what I'm not able to do."

Many of the suggestions for healthy mental living that psychologists, doctors, and counselors offer are found in Scripture. The recovering addict needs to know that God is a comfort and not a killjoy, one who will bring love, acceptance, and forgiveness and not blame and shame. Almost every addict we have worked with already understands the judgment of God. Hope comes from knowing a God of acceptance and forgiveness.

God loves us and wants us to reach our full potential. He accepts us despite our faults and failures. A recovering addict may be heartened to realize that King David, who was an adulterer and a murderer, repented of his sins and was called a man after God's own heart! God deeply loves each of us in spite of our sinful imperfections. No sin is too great because "nothing can come between us and the love of God."

Through the Bible, God continually demonstrates that He is the designer and builder of human life and understands what's best for us:

- Jesus was the first person in the Bible to suggest living one day at a time.
- Long before stress became a part of the twentieth-century vocabulary, the Bible urged readers to cast their cares and anxieties on the Lord because He cares for every person.
- Before "garbage in, garbage out" became a popular expression, the apostle Paul wrote in Philippians 4:8, "Whatever is true, whatever is noble, whatever is right, whatever is pure, whatever is lovely, whatever is admirable—if anything is excellent or praiseworthy—think about such things."

Summary

We have watched thousands of parents and teenagers struggle with substance abuse. Too many waited until their problems were unbearable before beginning the journey toward recovery. There's hope for winning the drug war in our land. That hope is in our hands—and in the hands of countless parents like you. The sooner we parents accept the challenge, the greater the possibility we can achieve positive change.

Every day, children in this country must make decisions about drugs. The only question is which decision they will make. Parents who do nothing to help their kids make that decision—who merely hope for the best, who blithely assume their kids are immune—are abandoning their children at the edge of an abyss of terror and death. Please be assured that your child doesn't have to enter that chasm of despair. You are competent to gather the resources to handle the problem. It is your responsibility. Please don't expect someone else to do it for you—and your child.

If your child is already involved with the dark side of adolescence, you can make a difference! It's not too late to make the tough decisions that will bring him or her back from the path of self-destruction.

CHAPTER SEVEN

Sexual Abuse

Jim will never forget how a simple meeting with a concerned parent changed his life forever. Janet sat in his office and said, "I've read all your material on sexuality that parents and churches use for discussion with their kids. You did a great job." There was a long pause, and then she continued, "However, your material on sexual abuse is very poor. I'm not sure you know much about the subject."

Now Jim paused. "You're right," he answered. "Very honestly, I don't know much about the subject."

She then said, "Do you know that many of those precious young girls in your youth group will be sexually abused by the age of 18 and that more of those boys than you can imagine will be abused as well?"

He wanted to say, "No way. You're absolutely wrong. You don't know my kids." But he didn't say anything. It was time to listen.

Janet, whose daughter had been sexually abused by a Christian high school teacher, was now on a personal mission to help abused kids and their families. Jim told her that only a few times in his 15-plus years of youth ministry had a young person ever brought up the subject of sexual abuse.

"How many times," she asked, "have you spoken on the subject or taught a curriculum on sexual abuse?"

He had to admit that he had never once discussed it.

Janet looked him straight in the eye and said, "I challenge you to talk about it soon with your youth group. In fact, I'll write the talk." (Jim liked that.) She then added, "But get ready for a life-changing experience."

A few weeks later, he gave his first presentation on sexual abuse to 400 students. Within the week, he talked to 27 of those kids about their sexual abuse. A floodgate had opened, and it has never stopped. Today, both of us realize that whenever we bring up the subject of sexual abuse—in a Christian youth gathering, church, or a public school assembly— listening kids will have shared the pain and horror of their own victimization through sexual abuse.

Janet was right. Jim's life will never be the same. For some reason, many parents, especially Christians, believe that "it won't happen to our family." Unfortunately, far too many parents unwisely believe that their children are immune from the pain of our world. Parents can help prevent sexual abuse in their family by becoming more informed.

What Is Sexual Abuse?

Sexual abuse occurs when a person is tricked, coerced, seduced, intimidated, forced, or manipulated into sexual activity with another person. Nontouching sexual activity or experiences include:

- showing children pornographic material
- taking nude pictures of children
- an adult exposing himself/herself to a child or asking the child to expose himself/herself

Touching sexual activity or experiences include:

- fondling private areas of a person's body
- genital contact
- intercourse
- rape

The most common type of sexual abuse among teens is "acquaintance rape" or "date rape." Date rapists, who generally use just enough force to gain compliance, are seldom weird, easily identifiable, or negative. They are just like anyone else, except they use force to get their way. About 75 percent of teen rapes are acquaintance or date rapes.

The Facts

At least one out of four girls and one out of eight boys will be sexually abused before age 18. Sexual abuse affects millions of innocent children. Even with the almost 1,000 percent increase in reported crimes of sexual abuse during the past 10 years, authorities tell us that only one out of 20 cases is ever reported. What some parents, pastors, and educators don't understand is that 80 percent of all sexual abuse cases involve adults our children know—often adults they love and trust.

Sara's father was a Bible study teacher at church. The congregation considered him to be a leader and a positive influence in the community. No one but Sara knew about his other life. Often he would fight with Sara's mother at night. He would then walk out of his bedroom and into Sara's room. Perhaps once a week, he would sleep with Sara in her single bed. When she was nine, he began to fondle her. But when she was 10, he started forcing her to have intercourse. He called it "our little secret." Sara remembers times when her father would sexually abuse her and then go teach his Bible study. If her mother knew, she never acknowledged that she did.

At age 11, Tom first went camping with his favorite uncle. Seven years later, he told his terrible story of forced homosexual rape that had been going on since their first camping trip.

Linda's stepbrother forced her to watch hours of the raunchiest pornographic films possible. He tried to "act out" those films with her, but, thank God, he was caught before he physically harmed her. However, the sexual abuse that had taken place left a deep scar in Linda's life. She told Jim, "I don't think I can ever get those pictures out of my mind. I'm not sure I can ever have a normal, healthy physical relationship with a man. Those pictures haunt me."

Cheryl, age 16, went to the prom with Bill, who was a year older. Cheryl's mother thought Bill was a "nice young man" and was pleased that they were double-dating because it was "safer." The expensive dinner and prom were wonderful. Bill was a perfect gentleman. But after the dance, Bill dropped the other couple off first and then "parked" with Cheryl. She was ecstatic from the thrills of the evening, and the passionate kissing was just one more highlight. His hands began to wander, however, and before she knew it he was taking off her clothes and his own. She tried to stop him, but she couldn't. "After all," she said later, "he spent a lot of money on our date." What Cheryl will remember most about her first prom was that she was raped.

Those stories break our hearts. At New Life Clinics and the National Institute of Youth Ministry, we hear such stories nearly every day.

Who Are These Abusers?

In the state of California, there are more than 64,000 registered sex offenders. Often sexual abusers look and act the same way as their neighbors.

Appearing to be normal, sexual abusers are not easily identifiable, and no one may know about their sexual addictions and abuses.

George (name changed) is a fairly typical child sex abuser. His daughter, Teri (name changed), was in Jim's youth group. Adopted at birth, she was a good kid who had a real desire to grow in her Christian faith. Eventually her parents got a divorce.

Years later, Teri told her psychologist that she had few childhood memories. (Often when people have memory blocks, it means that something traumatic happened to them during those years. In simple terms, their brains shut the painful memories out of their conscious minds.) The counselor then helped Teri recall some of the horrible abuse she suffered at her father's hands. Over the course of two years, Teri's counselor did an excellent job of helping Teri deal with this trauma in her life. Her counselor became her advocate and helped Teri develop an important support system.

When Teri explained some of the characteristics and conditions of her family, everything began to make sense. George had sexually molested other children. He had a history of depression and was raised in an unhappy home where quite possibly he was abused as a child. He was drunk most of the week. Teri's parents worked different shifts, were seldom at home at the same time, and were always under financial stress. Teri described her home with one word: "tension." Both parents suffered from low self-esteem and had little contact with other family members or friends.

After evaluating Teri's family life, it's easy to see that she was at much greater risk of sexual, physical, or emotional abuse than most children. Did her mother know the horror that went on? Teri believes the answer is yes. Her mother flatly denies it.

Does this mean that everyone who has had a traumatic childhood is a child abuser? Absolutely not! However, as parents today, we can't ignore the fact that child sexual abuse happens. Unfortunately, it happens in homes where we'd never dream it would take place.

You Can Make a Difference

As parents, our emphasis should be on reducing the risk of sexual abuse, not overcompensating with isolation. Sadly, child abuse is on the rise within youth groups, camps, and school situations. Here are some ways you can make a difference.

Evaluate Risk Factors

The best thing you can do is to become aware of the risk factors. The following list can help you be aware of persons outside your home who might be potential abusers. Again, we want to remind you that not every person who has one or more of these conditions is a sexual abuser.

• Has an unnatural interest in spending time with children.

- Doesn't have a caring relationship with another adult.
- Is addicted or abuses drugs or alcohol.
- Has a history of psychological problems, which may include previous sexual abuse.
- Was sexually abused as a child.
- Is presently using pornographic material.

Take Preventive Action

Having learned more about sexual abuse and counseled hundreds of victims as well as abusers, we now use much more caution with our own children. This means, for instance, that we want to know all of our baby-sitters. We ask our children questions about the baby-sitters' behavior. We ask other families about their experience with the sitter. If we ever have a "funny feeling," we don't use that sitter.

Our children don't have some freedoms others have when it comes to spending the night at a friend's house. We want to know the parents of our children's friends.

Without trying to be too overbearing, we try to meet youth group leaders, camp counselors, and basically anyone who will have the opportunity to spend individual time with our children. When we get that "funny feeling," we confront the person directly. If we sense something inconsistent in what the person is saying, we know we need to investigate further. If the person doesn't relate to kids the way others do, we are further alerted to a potential problem.

If we are not satisfied with the result of our

conversation, we will not entrust our children to the person or will talk to his or her supervisor. This lessens the chance of our children being victimized. Remember, family members or persons familiar to the family or child commit most acts of child abuse. We take this old adage to heart: "Better safe than sorry."

Warning Signs and Signals

One of our most important goals for this book is to help you reduce the risk of your children's being abused and to help you quickly detect warning signs. Most victims will not come to you right away with their secret. Teenagers and children may tell you something is wrong through their behavior rather than through their words. Listed below are a number of signals of sexual abuse. Again, however, the mere fact that a child displays one or more of these symptoms doesn't always mean that he or she has been sexually abused.

- poor peer relationships
- severe depression
- acting out sexual seduction
- fear or hostility of adults or a specific person
- running away
- pain or itching around the genitals
- nervous disorders
- withdrawn behavior
- regression to thumb-sucking or bed-wetting
- eating disorder

- nightmares or sleeping problems
- suicide attempts
- self-abuse behavior
- drug (including alcohol) abuse to cover the pain

Additional Tips on Preventing Child Sexual Abuse

Most children are taught to respect and obey adults. Of course, this proper teaching makes the prevention of child sexual abuse more difficult. You can, however, lessen the possibility of your children being sexually abused. They must be taught the following common principles at an early age. We recommend that you purchase some of the excellent age-appropriate books on prevention and read and discuss them with your children. Your Christian bookstore can guide you in the selection of appropriate books. You want to produce healthy respect in your children for their personhood, not deep-rooted fear.

1. It's okay to say no. Teach each of your children that it's absolutely fine to say no to an adult or even another child if your child doesn't feel right about what he or she is being asked to do. In our homes, we role-play situations and let our kids answer how they would respond. We have taught them never to accept rides, gifts, or favors from strangers.

2. If in doubt, stay away. Keep your kids away from situations where they may be around questionable persons. Help them understand that it's better to be safe than sorry. It's better to do something unpopular than regret making a decision for the sake of wanting to be liked. Once there was an instance in Jim's home when his daughter questioned out loud a friend's accidental touch. There was a very awkward moment and uncomfortable silence. Then the friend praised Jim's daughter for questioning his motives. She had been taught to question what she felt was inappropriate. Again we say, it's better to be safe than sorry.

3. Develop a "report-in" policy. As a parent, you shouldn't have to guess where your kids might be. A report-in policy simply states that whenever your kids change playmates, houses, school situations, parties—whenever they move from one place to another—they'll call you. Supply the coins, if necessary. In addition, it's vitally important for your kids to come straight home from school or the bus stop before going somewhere else.

4. Develop a trusting relationship with your kids. Make sure your kids know you will believe them if they report questionable behavior. Be their advocate. For instance, when Christy, Jim's daughter, was five, a little boy said and did things toward her that made Jim wonder if he had been abused. Jim listened to his daughter's story and immediately called the school principal. Your children need to know you'll plant yourself firmly on their side and not preach at them or question their integrity.

5. Participate in a child-sexual-abuse-awareness program in your school or community. Awareness reduces risk. Children and parents who know what to look for and what to do are better prepared to identify, stop, and report suspected child sexual abuse. Get involved with your local school and community to enhance awareness in your area. It's worth your time and energy. Do it for the kids.

This has not been a fun chapter to write and probably wasn't enjoyable to read. However, it's never too early for you to begin a prevention program with your children, and it's never too late to discuss the serious consequences of sexual abuse. Together, parents can make a difference in reducing the risk, trauma, and pain of our precious children being violated in ways that carry lasting scars.

CHAPTER EIGHT

Suicide

Carol's family perfectly illustrated a dysfunctional family. Her dad's life was out of control from too much work and too many affairs. Her mother, a submissive doormat/enabler, never missed church. Her sister rebelled through sexual promiscuity and drugs. Her brother shut down his emotions. Carol once said, "My brother is apathetic about everything but his television programs, which he watches eight hours a day."

Carol, on the other hand, was the family hero. Her good looks, outgoing personality, and beautiful smile won the hearts of everyone she met. She was the model everything: child, student, Christian. People often remarked, "Her family's a little weird, but Carol doesn't seem to be affected by their problems."

Then one day she snapped. Her boyfriend had

broken up with her over the weekend. Her world crumbled. She couldn't cope. Tired of pretending, she wanted to die. Sure, she had thought about suicide—"Doesn't everybody?" she had asked rhetorically at one point. But this time, she was serious. A deep, dark cloud filled her mind. Believing life was unbearable, she determined that her only option was to kill herself.

She decided to give life one more try, however. At school, she looked for Jerry, her former boyfriend. *If he will only pay attention to me or ask me out one more time,* she thought. All morning, she didn't see him. Then at lunch, she watched him put his arm around another girl as he had done with her a few days earlier. It was too much. Carol didn't even bother to pick up her books off the lunch table. She half walked, half ran to her car and bought two bottles of aspirin at the nearest drugstore. She then sped to a nearby park overlooking the Pacific Ocean. After praying and asking God to forgive her, she swallowed the contents of both bottles. It was the ultimate commentary on her messed-up family and messed-up world.

Carol woke up in the emergency ward of the local hospital and, having spent considerable time in counseling, today is helping other kids cope with their pain in more productive ways. Of course, Carol's story isn't as bleak as the stories of the five to seven thousand kids each year who aren't lucky enough to be found alive before it's too late.

Here are the facts:

- Adolescent suicide, the third leading cause of death for teenagers, has tripled during the past 30 years.
- Most teenagers think about suicide. Specifically, 73 percent have thought about committing suicide; 27 percent have actually tried to kill themselves.
- More females than males attempt suicide; however, more males than females die from suicide.
- Suicidal teenagers are more likely than others to have experienced: parental loss prior to age 12; physical or sexual abuse; a family characterized by talk of parents' divorce or separation; a family with a history of depression; and a parent who was chronically ill.

Far too often, parents, teachers, and youth workers don't learn enough about suicide until after a crisis. In our "Kids in Crisis" seminars, we routinely ask youth workers, parents, and pastors how many of them have been involved in a suicide-related situation during the previous year. Typically, at least three-quarters of the people raise their hands. The attendees often are motivated to learn more, because during a crisis they realized they didn't recognize the signs of suicidal risk.

Without a doubt, suicide is a sobering topic. Few people desire to become "experts" on this subject. But for the sake of your children, we want to give you an overview so you can recognize the warning signs before it's too late.

Common Myths About Suicide

Even people within the helping professions may hold common misunderstandings about suicide. The following myths will help you better understand some of the issues.

Myth #1: Suicide Occurs Without Warning

Not only do most suicidal people give warning, but they usually give multiple warnings. Unfortunately, it's easier to recognize the warnings after someone makes a suicide attempt. The following signs may indicate a risk of suicide. If a young person displays one, two, or more of these, it doesn't necessarily mean he or she will attempt suicide. It does mean, however, that his or her risk of suicide is high.

Emotional warning signs of suicide risk:

acute anger	daydreaming
irritability	shame
apathy	low self-esteem
guilt	frustration
moodiness	grief
hopelessness	passiveness
despair	bitterness
sadness	boredom
hypersensitivity	

Behavioral warning signs of suicide risk:

recklessness
risk-taking
eating disorders

self-destructive behavior
loss of interest in school, sports, hobbies,
   social activities
prone to accidents
alcohol and drug abuse
bed-wetting
cruelty
loss of interest in personal hygiene
changes in eating or sleeping habits
chain-smoking
social isolation
studying or talking about death and suicide
running away

Situational warning signs of suicide risk:

sexual, physical, or emotional abuse
suicide among friends
parental divorce
family violence or tension
family history of suicide
breakup with boyfriend or girlfriend
listening to music that romanticizes suicide
moving or changing schools
personal health problems
physical hardship or handicap
expulsion from school

Myth #2: People Who Talk About Suicide Won't Do It

The truth is that 80 percent of those who commit suicide *did* talk about it, but the people with whom they talked probably didn't take the warning seriously. Anyone talking about suicide should be taken seriously. Many parents are afraid that mentioning the idea of suicide will give their children the idea. That's not true. If you suspect a child is considering suicide, ask him or her.

A depressed girl came to Jim recently to talk about a breakup with her boyfriend, her parents' separation, and her sexual promiscuity. During the conversation, Jim said, "You've really had a rough few months. Some people in your situation might think about suicide. Does that ever cross your mind?" The young woman nodded her head yes. Jim talked to the girl about her suicidal thoughts, and she concluded that although her life was difficult, suicide wasn't the answer.

Myth #3: Suicidal People Don't Seek Medical Help

Research shows that three out of four people visited a doctor for some physical complaint within one to three months before taking their lives. The reasons for the visit varied from extreme emotional problems to something as simple as a common cold.

Myth #4: All Suicidal People Are Mentally Ill

Too many people believe that suicide happens only to those who are mentally ill, mentally retarded, or very poor. They can't imagine that normal people would want to take their lives. The truth is, however, that only 15 percent of those who take their lives have actually been diagnosed as being mentally ill. Most of the time, people considering suicide appear normal to people around them.

Myth #5: Suicidal People Are Totally Committed to Dying

One of the most common characteristics of adolescents who are contemplating suicide is ambivalence. They have a strong desire to end their lives, but at the same time, they strongly desire to live. Your best approach is to use their ambivalence to encourage their strong feelings about living. To be safe, if a child reaches this point of despair, you should have him or her under the care of a trained professional.

Myth #6: When the Depression Lifts, the Suicide Crisis Is Over

Often the lifting of depression means only that the adolescent has finally decided to take his or her own life. Once the decision has been made, depression is often replaced with a feeling of euphoria or relief. Many suicides occur within three months after the victims have appeared to overcome their depression. That is why kids who obtain treatment need to continue in an after-care program and ongoing therapy.

Needed: Time, Place, and Method

Although any person's mention of suicide should be taken seriously, there are (at the risk of being overly blunt) three things needed in order for someone to commit suicide: a time, a place, and a method.

A distraught young man Jim had previously known from a youth group called him one day. Jim hadn't seen or heard from him for at least seven years.

After identifying himself, he asked, "Is this the Jim Burns who used to be my youth minister?"

"You're talking to him," Jim said.

The next words out of his mouth changed the tone of the conversation: "I'm planning on killing myself tonight."

Jim first reassured him that he remembered him and that he cared. Then he simply asked the young man how, when, and where he planned to do it.

He had the answers no one on the other end of the line wants to hear. "I've got a gun loaded in my drawer. I want to get blitzed (drunk) and shoot myself in my bedroom listening to the Beatles singing 'Eleanor Rigby.'"

No doubt about it; he was serious. Jim needed to assist him immediately. He agreed to meet Jim at a local restaurant, and after several hours of discussion, they both went back to his apartment. The young man removed the weapon, and Jim drove him to a treatment center, where he received needed attention for the issues that led him to seriously consider suicide.

Sometimes kids will think about suicide but really haven't worked through the details. These kids are still very much at risk and need help, although their situations may not be as critical as that of Jim's friend from the old youth group.

The following questionnaire, designed by A. G.

Devries and published in Keith Olson's excellent book, *Counseling Teenagers*, provides a quick "suicide potential" evaluation based on the person's self-rating:

		Yes	No
1.	My future happiness looks promising.	☐	☐
2.	I have recently had difficulty sleeping.	☐	☐
3.	I think I am to blame for almost all my troubles.	☐	☐
4.	When I'm sick, the doctor often prescribes sedatives for me.	☐	☐
5.	Sometimes I really feel afraid.	☐	☐
6.	Sometimes I fear I will lose control over myself.	☐	☐
7.	Lately, I haven't felt like participating in my usual activities.	☐	☐
8.	I go on occasional drinking sprees.	☐	☐
9.	In the last few years, I have moved at least twice.	☐	☐
10.	I have someone whose well-being I care about very much.	☐	☐
11.	I generally feel completely worthless.	☐	☐
12.	I frequently have a drink in the morning.	☐	☐

Suicidal counselees will tend to produce the following pattern of responses:

1. No	5. Yes	9. Yes
2. Yes	6. Yes	10. No
3. Yes	7. Yes	11. Yes
4. Yes	8. Yes	12. Yes [1]

What to Do If Your Child Is Suicidal

Seek Help

This isn't a time to play "armchair psychologist." A suicidal child needs an assessment from a trusted professional. We strongly urge you to seek out someone in your community who is knowledgeable in the area of suicide and get his or her opinion. If you can't find help in your area, call one of the national crisis hot lines listed in the back of this book or the New Life Clinics' free counseling service at 1/800/332-TEEN. They can help you get immediate assistance.

Remain Calm and Positive

We're aware of a father who went "berserk" when his daughter showed him a bottle of sleeping pills she planned to swallow. His anger and negative behavior encouraged her to later swallow the pills. She didn't die, but she was making what professionals call a "suicide gesture." The purpose of such a gesture is to emphasize an emotional statement by directly flirting with death. Kids who make suicide gestures are emphasizing the depth of their pain and problems. Parents of suicidal children need to remain calm and positive and get the children immediate help before their gestures become actual suicide attempts.

Stay in Touch

When your young person is suicidal, it's very important to keep in touch often, monitor his or her emotional stability, and stay in contact physically.

The warmth of a hug does wonders for calming a child who doesn't feel loved.

Don't Get into a Philosophical Debate

This is a time to show care, empathy, and love toward your child. It's not the time to discuss the ever-asked question: "Can a person commit suicide and still go to heaven?" It's not the time to belittle or shame, either.

Take Away the Suicide Method

Always try to remove whatever your child plans to use to kill himself or herself. But never try to physically remove a weapon from your child. Manipulate it away instead. This means you must talk it out of his or her hands, rather than knock it out or grab it. The best advice in this situation is to not panic, even though on the inside you're tense. Someone—namely you—needs to be in control.

Pray

Prayer works. In addition to being a means by which you can communicate with God, prayer can give you a proper perspective. We often ask if we can pray with a young person who is considering suicide. Prayer calms suicidal people and brings them toward God—the real source of hope and healing.

You Can Make a Difference

Although not the only factor in determining the risk of suicide, the family unit is the major factor in reducing the risk of suicide. Following are several ways in which you can help children reduce the possibility of ever having to deal with suicide.

Teach and Encourage Your Children to Communicate Openly

Kids need an open environment—a safe place— in which to discuss problems and concerns, to raise questions, and to talk through doubts. Kids who are raised in an open environment are much less likely to suffer from trapped feelings and are more likely to find solutions to their problems. An open atmosphere at home will help children develop a positive self-image. We often tell parents to devote special time and attention to each child so he or she will feel loved and cared for as an individual. Kids who feel good about themselves and feel loved are much less likely to become depressed or suicidal.

Teach and Model Healthy Ways to Handle Stress

Children tend to copy the behaviors of parents and other significant adults. When kids learn that stress is part of life and develop healthy ways to deal with it, they are better able to handle problems throughout their lives. Family life is never easy, yet one of our key parenting roles must be to develop and maintain stable home environments with healthy family relationships. Children's depression and suicide risk are directly related to family problems.

Jim is from a family where some members, at one

time in their lives, handled stress by numbing their pain with alcohol. As a result, he and his wife are more aware of how they handle stress. So his daughters, Christy, Rebecca, and Heidi, are three reasons Jim doesn't drink. Jim knows that children do what they see.

Monitor Your Kids' Emotional and Behavioral Changes

Kids often express frustrations through emotional outbursts or altered behavioral patterns. Also, children sometimes become depressed or suicidal as a response to what's happening within their peer group, so it's good to know your kids' friends and their behaviors. We have both chosen to make our homes a meeting place where our children's friends can hang out. It's partly a selfish motivation; we want to keep better tabs on who our children's friends are and how they cope with life.

Keep Alcohol, Medications, Guns, Knives, and Other Potentially Dangerous Objects Locked Away from Children

We've seen too many kids attempt suicide as an impulsive response to depression or a crisis. We know a family in which a grandmother kept a loaded gun under her bed in case of a break-in. Everyone knew where the gun was and was told never to touch it. One day, her depressed grandson broke into her home and used the gun on himself. That family will never be the same. You can never know how long someone might obsessively think about the hidden weapon in your home. A suicide that appears impulsive might be the result of months or years of focusing on the object of self-destruction.

Help Children Realize That Death Is Permanent

Many children, especially those under age 12, don't understand the finality of death. They may even believe that death is reversible. While emphasizing the permanence of death, also emphasize the temporary nature of a child's problems. Suicide is a permanent response to a temporary problem.

We couldn't end this chapter without emphasizing again how important it is to seek professional help if your child appears to be suicidal. Counseling can uncover the cause of your child's problem and develop an approach to resolve it before your child takes life-threatening actions.

CHAPTER NINE

Satanism

The horrors of Satanism are so terrible that some people even deny the existence of this dangerous trend. To know it's real, you only have to walk the halls of a prison, a psychiatric institution, or even most high schools in America. Satanists in our schools wear jewelry with goats' heads and penta-grams on their clothes. Upside-down crosses and 666 are other symbols found on their clothes and posses-sions. More often than not, they listen to heavy-metal music whenever possible. These kids have escaped into the ultimate underworld of power and deceit. They can be brought back, but it's never easy.

Fourteen-year-old Tommy Sullivan didn't make it back. His is not only a modern-day horror story, but it also made the headlines of every major newspaper a few years ago.

Tommy came from a Christian home in Sparta, New Jersey. He had attended Catholic schools since first grade, along with his brother, Brian, who was four years younger. Tommy was an average student who loved sports and who cut grass and shoveled snow to earn spending money. A mild-mannered kid, he occasionally got into mischief but never any serious trouble. Tall and athletic, he excelled at wrestling and had already won several awards.

His father, Thomas Sr., was a medical-supplies salesman. He took a genuine interest in his boys, frequently playing softball and basketball with them or working alongside them to build model airplanes or fix bicycles.

Tommy's 37-year-old mother, Bettyanne, was a year younger than her husband. She was a full-time wife and mother. Devoted to her kids and her faith, Bettyanne sent her sons to Catholic schools so they would receive a good education instilled with moral values. She volunteered her time as a school aide and as a Cub Scout den mother.

Although on the surface the family members seemed to be doing just fine, they were the ultimate dysfunctional family. Thomas Sr. was a strict disciplinarian; Bettyanne exhibited compulsive behavior. Her house was immaculate, and she demonstrated great control and overinvolvement in her sons' lives. As strict as Thomas Sr. was about discipline and obedience, he believed the boys needed more breathing room than his wife was giving. But both parents agreed that the boys needed to obey them without questioning.

By junior high, Tommy was exhibiting a slightly rebellious streak. He started talking back to his parents and was especially vocal about not wanting to go to church or the parochial junior high. The school he attended required uniforms that made him feel uncomfortably "different" from all the neighborhood public school kids. He longed for the easier life at public schools.

When he entered eighth grade, Tommy seemed different to his teachers and friends—more distant, sullen, uptight, and tight-lipped. He could hide his feelings from his teachers, but his buddies knew that he was doing a slow burn inside in response to his parents' strictness. During the first semester, Tommy's religion class touched on a number of religions and cults prevalent in modern society, one of which was satanism. Tommy was aghast at the idea and was quoted by classmates as saying the whole idea was "weird and scary." But perhaps aspects of satanism intrigued him—the offer of ultimate power and revenge. At any rate, he devoted an entire paper to satanism, for which he earned an A.

When Tommy began to go regularly to the public library to obtain books on satanism, witchcraft, and the occult, his parents thought it was just a superficial, passing interest. He continually shut himself in his room, obsessed with listening to heavy-metal rock bands like Ozzy Osbourne and Mötley Crüe, whose songs included lyrics about suicide and killing one's mother. His parents thought he was just going through a rebellious phase. When Tommy encouraged his friends to join his "club" to worship the devil, they thought he was just trying to get attention. As he became more withdrawn, however, his friends became more bewildered. Like his classmates, Tommy kept a school journal in which he entered feelings, impressions, and thoughts. Unlike those of his classmates, though, Tommy's journal was filled with satanic drawings and verbiage, including vows to the devil that he would kill his parents.

On Tuesday, January 5, 1988, Tommy told his best friend that Satan had instructed him in a dream to kill his mother and father within 10 years. On January 7, acting on a tip from one of Tommy's friends, the principal of Tommy's school, Sister Philomena, held a conference with Mrs. Sullivan. The principal showed her notes in Tommy's handwriting with coded messages and satanic symbols. Mrs. Sullivan was not concerned and assured Sister Philomena that her son was just into a passing phase.

Concerned about his son's increasingly taciturn nature and withdrawal from family and friends, however, Thomas Sr. realized it was important for him to spend more one-on-one time with Tommy. So he took Tommy to a wrestling match (his favorite sport) at the local high school on Saturday afternoon. When they returned home, Mr. Sullivan went to bed, feeling that he was coming down with influenza.

About 10:30 that night, a smoke alarm went off. Mr. Sullivan raced into the living room along with his younger son, Brian, and discovered a small fire.

As they were putting it out, they saw someone drive off in the family car, plow it into a snowbank down the street, and run away. Confused and concerned, Mr. Sullivan ran to a neighbor's house, where he called the police. Returning home with a neighborhood friend of Tommy's, Mr. Sullivan and Brian began searching the house for his wife and older son. They found Mrs. Sullivan in the basement. Her face had been grotesquely mutilated, and her throat had been slit.

Mr. Sullivan called the police again. They didn't find Tommy that night, but they did find his clothes, an inverted cross, and a note addressed to the "greatest demons of hell" inside the car. The note included the vow to kill his family within 10 years, which was now crossed out with the words, "I have already killed my family."

The next morning, Tommy was found dead in the snow in a neighbor's backyard. With his Boy Scout knife, he had slit his wrists and cut his throat from ear to ear. Tommy's father still grieves the loss of his wife and son. His pain is hard to handle, and his depression grows more intense each day.

What Is Satanism?

Tommy's father isn't alone in his grief over such senseless loss. Others have lost children and entire families to something they may not even have known existed. Satanism—the worship of Satan—does exist. Followers of Satan believe he can and will give them power in exchange for their allegiance. They take to heart the exact opposite of the Judeo-Christian philosophy as expressed in the golden rule. Instead of suppressing their pleasure for the welfare of others, satanists believe in doing whatever they want, whenever they want. In short, they become a law unto themselves for their own purposes, often for pleasure or revenge.

Alarming Facts

Walter Martin, author of *The Kingdom of the Cults*, defines a cult "as a group of people gathered about a specific person or person's misinterpretation of the Bible." He further states that there are over 20 million cult members in the United States alone. The Cult Awareness Network (CAN), which is based in Chicago, reports that calls on satanism alone have increased 300 percent from just three years ago. They now receive several hundred calls on satanism per month. A *Seventeen* magazine survey found that 12 percent of American teenagers have "some or a lot of faith in satanism." [1]

According to research conducted by Texas A&M University in College Station, Texas, police officers believe that satanism is responsible for one in 10 homicides and one in three suicides in teens. [2]

Young Men at Risk

Some researchers estimate that 5 percent of all adolescents are involved in satanism to some degree. Most of those are males. That's a large enough number to put parents on the alert. If satanism were considered a disease, it would be an epidemic. Johanna Michaelson, in her book *Like Lambs to a Slaughter,* profiles young people who are attracted to the occult:

> Satanism is the ultimate in rebellion. It carries a "blood-and-guts" macho image that generally (but by no means exclusively) appeals to boys. The typical teenage Satan-worshiper tends to be a creative and intelligent white male from a middle- to upper-class family. He probably is an underachiever and has a poor self-image.
>
> He likely feels alienated from his family and traditional values and religious beliefs, as well as feeling conflict in his relationships with his peers. He is bored and desperately looking for something new and exciting to fill the emptiness of his existence. "What have I got to live for?" is a question he may be asking. His life is characterized by a sense of personal helplessness.[3]

This troubled teenager has few friends and many family conflicts. He is creative, curious, and has a low self-esteem. He is attracted to satanism because it offers what he is missing in life—friends, power, prestige, and the ability to control his life or other people's lives. He is drawn by the possibilities of sex, drugs, recognition, and respect. In other words, he is an already troubled youth before he discovers satanism.

Sandi Gallant, a San Francisco police officer who investigates ritualistic crimes, makes it clear that satanism is symptomatic "of a mind bent on destroying. If the kid did not grow into satanism, he would have found drugs, alcohol, or some other kind of excuse for his bad behavior."[4] She adds that if a teenager entertains suicidal or homicidal tendencies, satanism may be the catalyst that sets him off.

The Four Categories of Satanists

If a child becomes involved with satanism, the progression of involvement is similar to that of drug addiction. Early intervention is important to prevent a slight fascination from becoming an all-consuming obsession. Those knowledgeable about cults and the occult generally break down satanists into four categories.

Traditional or Religious Satanists

These include people like Anton La Vey, author of *The Satanic Bible*. He started the Church of Satan, which openly worships the devil, in 1966, the year he decreed to be Year One of the Satanic Age. He and his followers are open about their practice and worship of Satan in a church service—the Black Mass, which is the antithesis of the Catholic Mass. They claim to be firmly opposed to illegal activities. They intellectually reject Christianity and all it stands for and claim to have nothing to do with animal or human sacrifices.

Outlaw and Intergenerational Satanists

These are small, secret cult organizations that are not well known outside their members.

"Outlaw Satanists," small cults usually organized around drug use or sex, participate in such illegal activities as robbing homes and stealing to support their activities. These groups are also involved in the mutilation of animals and desecration of churches. Surprisingly, doctors, lawyers, and other community leaders are sometimes secret members of these groups.

Intergenerational satanists are a relatively small but secretive group in which the "religion" is passed on from each generation. Members of this family religion are literally born into the cult; some may actually attend Christian churches.

Experimental Satanists

Millions of Americans dabble in the occult, witchcraft, and even devil worship without actually being committed satanists. This category includes teenagers who are intrigued by horror movies, hard-rock bands that specialize in satanic themes, and people who act out certain fantasy games such as Dungeons & Dragons in which elements of magic and witchcraft are an integral part of the action.

Self-Styled Satanists

If experimental satanists become more deeply involved, they usually move into this category. Self-styled satanists basically borrow satanic themes, symbols, and other elements to support a belief system they have created for themselves and practice by themselves. A mass murderer like Richard Ramirez, the "Night Stalker," was probably already mentally disturbed before adopting satanic symbolism and culture. Mental illness feeds satanic beliefs, and satanic beliefs feed mental illness. Both are based on delusion; and although all mentally ill people aren't involved in satanism, there are often satanic themes in their delusions.

You Can Make a Difference

Your child may read books on satanism and the occult out of a morbid curiosity. That is not unusual. However, you should be concerned if your child exhibits signs of isolation and low self-esteem.

Warning Symptoms

As in drug addiction, none of the following symptoms by itself is a sure indicator of satanism. Several of them combined, however, make a pattern similar to that of other young people who either dabble in or are profoundly entrenched in satanism. Immediately take notice if your child exhibits several of the following:

- significant drop in grades
- withdrawal from family and old friends
- mood swings
- dropping favorite sports and activities and not replacing them with other meaningful hobbies
- "lashing out" in anger, especially over seemingly trivial matters

- secretive or elusive behavior
- radical changes in eating and/or sleeping patterns

Parents should immediately be suspicious if their teenager exhibits the following signs or behaviors:

- reads the Book of Shadows, a small journal with a black cover that teenagers keep as a diary. Here they put notes, drawings, spells, instructions for rituals, letters to the devil, and pacts with Satan.
- has pentagrams drawn on his or her hands or possessions.
- is obsessed with "black" heavy-metal bands, especially those that promote satanic themes. AC/DC and Ozzy Osbourne are no longer involved with the occult, but many such as Venom, Slayer, Judas Priest, WASP, Dio, Black Sabbath, and Led Zeppelin have strong satanic themes. King Diamond is an admitted satanist; his rock concerts highlight an altar to Satan and a coffin.
- uses any of the following occult symbols: pentagrams, upside-down crosses, swastikas, or daggers dripping blood.
- has painted pinky finger or middle finger on the left hand black or red.
- has draped his bedroom in black gauze and/or painted or hung any occult symbolism on the walls.
- has built black altars.

Take Satanism Seriously

Experts on cults and the occult agree that parents should never take their children's interest in satanism lightly. Never dismiss it as a phase he or she will grow out of. If your child is interested in reading books on occult subjects, read and discuss the material with him or her. Listen to what your child is saying, and evaluate it in terms of identifying occult themes that appeal to young people.

The existence of paraphernalia, dress, and symbols of the occult is a sign that your child needs tremendous help. Some of the bizarre behavior is actually a cry for help. You should move quickly to seek counsel from those who have worked with kids involved with the occult. Don't wait. This problem will most likely become worse if you do. The homicidal and suicidal potential that goes with satanism should seriously motivate you to act quickly and wisely.

If you've seen some of these symptoms exhibited in your children or are worried about some of the issues mentioned here, it would be wise to seek counsel from your pastor or a family counselor. (If your child is a satanist, he or she will probably resent a pastor being involved, so a counselor may seem more neutral and be able to produce results more quickly.) The counselor will try to connect with the child's sense of hopelessness or driving thirst for power, knowledge, and/or revenge. If the counselor can get your child talking, there's potential to get to the roots of the child's rebellion and heal the relationship between you and your child. This isn't a quick process, and it'll require tough work—especially from you.

Hope

As parents, all of us should be worried about our children's involvement with satanism. However, we should be encouraged, too, that no matter how deep our children may be into the occult, there is real hope through concern, action, and prayer. The Bible gives us comforting words when it comes to our struggle against Satan: "Our struggle is not against flesh and blood, but against the rulers, against the authorities, against the powers of this dark world and against the spiritual forces of evil in the heavenly realms" (Eph. 6:12, NIV).

The hope that Christian parents can hold on to is spelled out clearly in the New Testament: "The reason the Son of God appeared was to destroy the devil's work" (1 John 3:8, NIV).

The battle for a child's soul is never easy, and if your child is involved in satanic practices, the battle will be especially difficult. You'll need to use all the resources available to you to win. This is a supernatural battle with supernatural powers.

Prayer is one of the greatest resources at your disposal. We have seen miraculous things happen to children whose parents refused to give up on prayer. Prayer is the power that places the armor of God within reach of your child and God's armor is sufficient for your child. Don't think us strange or weird, but when it comes to dealing with satanism, you must be willing to fight this awful spiritual battle on a spiritual plane as well as a physical one.

We cannot promise that if you are faithful to the Lord, your child will make it out of a cult or forsake Satan worship. There are no guarantees. But this is your only hope. Do not give up. There can be a great victory when our Lord is in the battle.

CHAPTER TEN

Homosexuality

Let's get something straight from the beginning of this chapter. An almost panicked feeling comes over parents whenever they must deal with their children's sexual identity issues. Parents hope and pray that their children will grow up "normal." They hope and pray that each child will find the perfect mate with whom to walk down the path of marital bliss. And most parents hope their children will, in turn, produce "Kodak-picture-perfect" children. Unfortunately, that doesn't always happen.

To some of you, the information we present here will be extremely controversial. From our experiences, however, this approach to the difficult problem of homosexuality offers the greatest hope for parents and their children. We have counseled many Christian parents who were brokenhearted over the sexual-preference decisions their children had made. The revelation to Christian parents that their child is having a homosexual relationship is perhaps more painful than any other problem they could face. Maybe it's because homosexuality involves the adolescent's entire identity. Or it could be because children who move into a homosexual lifestyle abandon so many values their Christian parents hold dear.

One reason homosexual children create such pain is that many parents see their children's decision as the worst sin possible. They don't view it the same way as they view adultery, gossip, or stealing. Many parents believe homosexuality to be the sign of a heart that has turned completely against God. In dealing with these families, we've tried to help but have made little progress with many who didn't want to understand the problem. Either they wanted the adolescents to change or they wanted to deny the problem existed.

Our purpose in the next few pages is to help parents handle homosexuality from a perspective of understanding. Once the problem is understood, there's a much greater chance of communicating with adolescents involved in homosexual behavior.

Homosexuality is another family problem that we approach from more than a textbook understanding. Steve's brother, Jerry, was a practicing homosexual for many years. Jerry's struggle in going against what he believed was right and later returning to his conservative Christian values has taught us much. The struggle of Mr. and Mrs. Arterburn to understand Jerry has also shown us that parents can continue to love their children even if those children turn away from them. Steve's parents have taught us, too, that the point at which it's most difficult to love a child is also the point at which the child needs love the most. That love can and needs to be given.

How Does Sexual Orientation Change?

To help you understand how some people become confused about their sexual orientation, we present the story of Grant. Through letters and phone conversations, we have confirmed that his story is typical of many who choose to lead a homosexual lifestyle.

Grant could have been "the boy next door." He came from a solid, respectable, Christian family that included a younger brother and two older sisters, two cats, and a dog. They lived in a large, midwestern city filled with parks, pools, playgrounds, and fine schools. Grant's father thought it would be a fine place to raise a family.

The children were all personable, bright, and excellent students at the nondenominational Christian academy they attended. Grant's father worked in the aeronautics industry as a consultant. He had started out as a career U.S. Air Force man in Texas, but civilian opportunities opened up that allowed him to keep his military pension. His wife worked part-time, teaching drama classes to junior high students at the academy. She enjoyed her role as a loyal wife and full-time mother.

The family's fair-sized church had an active

congregation. Choir practices, church picnics, Wednesday night "Study of the Word" meetings, Vacation Bible School, and family retreats were all part of the family's activities.

Grant was completing fourth grade when the middle school boys' choir was invited to sing at an Easter-week rally in a nearby city. The kids were going to perform at a civic auditorium and would stay overnight in a local church that was involved with the program.

At age 10, Grant hardly knew what the show was all about. But he enthusiastically poked and punched the other boys backstage and sang with gusto "This Little Light of Mine" when the troupe was on stage. Afterward there were punch and cookies for all, and then a ride to the church, where everyone pulled out sleeping bags to have a camp-out in the Sunday school classrooms.

Grant had just fallen soundly asleep when one of the adult sponsors at the host church shook his leg. Holding his finger to his mouth, the sponsor motioned Grant to keep quiet, then wiggled his finger for Grant to follow. Disoriented yet curious, Grant crawled out of his bag and went into one of the rooms down the hall.

The young man closed the door behind them without turning on the lights, then pulled Grant close to him in an embrace. After a few moments, he guided Grant's hand down on his genitals. "This is a very special time for us," the sponsor gushed. "Remember, we all love each other as Christians. We really do care about each other, and we need to share that with one another!" He reached down with his other hand and stroked Grant between the legs.

Grant was terrified. He knew the man was important, so what he was doing *couldn't* be wrong. Even though Grant vaguely felt a pleasant sensation, he couldn't feel good about it. Instinctively he knew the whole thing was wrong, wrong, wrong. He was afraid of pulling away to show his disapproval and kept hoping someone would walk by so the man would stop.

Finally, after what seemed to be an eternity, the man put both his arms around Grant and pressed him close. "This is our special time," the man whispered. "We must all show how we care for one another!" He loosened his grip and opened the door, and Grant ran back to his room.

Grant was panicked, afraid, and nauseated. He wanted fiercely to cry but was afraid the older boys would hear him and think he was a baby, worried about being away from home. He wanted desperately to go into the bathroom and scrub the memory of the man off his hands, his arms, his face, and even the back of his head. But he was terrified. Perhaps the man was there, waiting for him. He dared not go to sleep, either, for fear the man would return.

The next morning, Grant was overwhelmed with feelings of guilt and confusion. As he looked around the room, he tried to discern if the other boys could tell what had happened. Did they know? Could anyone else have gone through the same experience?

He avoided the other boys as they packed up their sleeping bags and got ready to eat breakfast.

In the multipurpose room where they gathered to eat, Grant saw the sponsor who had molested him. The man smiled at Grant as though he were any of the other visiting kids, giving no sign of recognition. *Is this supposed to happen?* Grant wondered. *Is it a normal thing to do? If I tell another adult, will I be in trouble? Why did that man want to touch me like that?*

During the ride home, Grant withdrew from the others while they horsed around. He knew that what he had experienced was wrong. The incident had propelled him into a new sphere of carnal knowledge that he couldn't comprehend. Back at home, Grant found himself too embarrassed to discuss the episode with his father, who just wasn't the sort to discuss feelings and private matters. Grant wondered if his mother would be too shocked. Would she be ashamed of him?

"One of the adult sponsors hugged me after the concert when we all went to bed," Grant said timidly when his mother asked about his concert.

"Oh, he must have been so proud of you!" she gushed. "We're all so very proud of you boys!"

"Well, yes, but . . . he did it differently!" Grant tried again. "And he didn't even know me!"

"I'm sure he knew you were one of the little boys who sang so well, honey. He doesn't have to know your individual names to recognize what a great job you all did!"

Grant nodded in agreement as he felt his head swim and his throat close up. He went upstairs to the bathroom and quietly wept with frustration from the burden of a secret he could never reveal. The guilt, the confusion, the embarrassment, and the inability to share made him feel terribly alone.

Throughout grade school and junior high, Grant looked back on that incident as an event that forever made him feel "different" and set apart. He continued to feel isolated and unaccepted, while at the same time longing desperately to be close to someone of the same sex. His obsessions turned into desire.

Initially, Grant would not have thought of a sexual attraction. He just ached to have a close male friend, one who would listen to him and love him. Only after high school did his feelings of alienation and loneliness bring him into a homosexual relationship.

Grant's story, sad to say, is not an isolated incident. It's printed here, not because of the event itself, but because of the way in which Grant thought he had to deal with it. This story points out more than just a sick adult youth leader who took advantage of a young boy. It points out subtle family relationships and how they affect a child's ability to handle life's tragedies.

Is Being Gay Okay?

This issue used to be simple from theological and psychological points of view. The field of psychiatry viewed homosexuality as a maladaptive lifestyle and treated it as a problem. Now many psychiatrists view it as nothing more than an alternate lifestyle, not an indication of underlying emotional problems. In many denominations, the church's view of homosexuality has also changed. Many denominations that used to interpret the Bible as condemning homosexual behavior now openly welcome homosexuals as ministers. This has produced a lot of confusion.

Major changes in the way homosexuality is viewed have also taken place in the political arena. In recent years, a strong gay-rights movement has emerged. Nearly every major city now celebrates a "gay pride" day. Some state legislatures have considered bills that would grant minority status to homosexuals—making it illegal even for churches and church-run organizations to discriminate against gays.

These trends have left many parents asking important questions that affect how we raise our children: "Is a homosexual lifestyle normal?" "Are evangelical Christians lacking insight into this problem, or are they right in holding on to their biblical view of homosexuality?" "Is homosexuality just an alternate lifestyle?" "What exactly is a homosexual?" "If children have homosexual tendencies, should parents make them feel more comfortable with their feelings or try to change the way they feel?"

Those are tough questions, and how we approach them has much to do with our conclusions. If we don't believe in absolute right and wrong, our minds are made up already. If we do believe in absolute right and wrong, our challenge is to develop a balanced response to this difficult problem.

Separating the Issues

In looking at homosexuality, each of us must carefully differentiate between the person and his or her behavior. To do this, we must consider homosexuality and homosexual behavior as two separate issues.

Homosexuality is an inclination or desire for someone of the same sex to provide emotional intimacy, acceptance, and/or affection. It describes the heart—the identity—of a person who isn't attracted to people of the opposite sex. It doesn't always result in homosexual behavior.

Homosexual behavior, on the other hand, is the manifestation of that inclination and desire. The difference is significant. Lust is a sin, but inclination toward lust is not. The inclination toward homosexuality is not a sin, but the behavior, as outlined in Scripture, is. Scripture is clear that homosexual behavior is sin. It is one of several sexual behaviors that are unacceptable to God. We are not to have sex with our parents, children, brothers, sisters, with animals, with another person's spouse, or with a person of the same sex.

Through the years, a number of groups have asserted that sex is permissible with any and all of the above. One group tried to convince the world that it's good for children to have sex with their parents. "Swingers" tried to convince others that sex with someone else's spouse is liberating. Groups who want to be free from the standards of God's Word are not new. The Bible clearly acknowledges that some people will desire to have sex with others of the same sex. It also clearly states that people so inclined are to abstain. Many people today say this is unreasonable. We believe it's a tough reality.

Many individuals make a sexual decision based on their theological beliefs. Dedicated nuns and priests, for instance, choose to not have sex out of commitment to God. A Christian man attracted to a woman who's not his wife must abstain if he's to remain true to his beliefs. A woman who kisses her soldier-husband good-bye must resist natural urges while he's away if she is to remain faithful to the God-ordained institution of marriage. Only an animal must give in to sexual urges. Human beings have the ability to make decisions that counter sexual urges.

When a married man is attracted to a woman other than his wife, that attraction isn't sinful. What the man does with that attraction, however, can become sin. Lusting after her—wanting her for sexual pleasure, fantasizing about her—is sin. Having sex with her is sinful. Sin comes from a decision to move beyond the attraction.

According to biblical standards, the same principle holds true for a homosexual. Sexual attraction to a person of the same gender isn't a sin. Heterosexuals don't lust after every person they're attracted to, and neither do homosexuals. But when homosexuals act on the attraction and sexualize it, according to Scripture they cross over a line into behavior that is not acceptable to God. As individuals, they are acceptable and deserving of our love. We must not reject them. It's their behavior that's sinful.

To have homosexual tendencies and to desire to not act on them is difficult in this society. Few voices say anything other than "Do what you feel like doing."

In 1 Corinthians 6:9-11, Paul spoke to Christians living in a perverse, pagan society that practiced (among other things) idol worship, homosexual behavior, and other sexual perversions. He clearly directed the Christians to separate themselves from those practices, saying that those who engage in them "will not inherit the kingdom of God." He also reminded believers that some of them had been involved in those behaviors before they committed their lives to Christ. Now they were to live differently. They were "washed . . . sanctified . . . justified" through Christ and by the Holy Spirit. Paul believed that through the power of Christ, anything that would further the glory of God was possible.

All of us must remind ourselves that we are capable of sinful behaviors such as these. Our hearts are sinful. In other words, all of us are born with the inclination to veer off the narrow path onto the broad road of sin. We must never view ourselves as spiritually superior to others. Only by our commitment to Christ, the grace of God, and the power of the Holy Spirit do we not fall into some of the sins Paul described.

"I've Been This Way Since I Can Remember"

One of the difficulties in reaching people involved in homosexual behavior is their deeply rooted feeling that they've been that way as long as they can remember. If we take the time to listen to what they really mean, we may be able to help.

First, homosexuals have not been having sex with people of the same gender since they were children (unless they were molested). Second, they haven't even been having sexual thoughts and feelings about others of the same gender since early childhood (again, unless they were molested or otherwise introduced to sexual behavior early on). In normal development, sexual urges come later.

So what do homosexuals mean when they say "I've been this way since I can remember"? They mean they've been different—they've had different feelings and wanted to do things that aren't always acceptable in our culture. They're describing early childhoods that left them feeling alone, alienated, and often rejected by those who should have loved them. It's not difficult to see how this could happen in our culture and many others.

The problem lies in what we accept as normal in our children. Boys who don't fit the norm are often called sissies. Girls who don't fit are called tomboys. These are obvious examples of how labels can be used to characterize children as different just because they have unique interests or talents. Not only do other kids make fun of them, but their parents often reject them as well by the way they treat them.

If a macho father who wants a football player for a son sees his young boy playing with dolls, he might shudder in fear that his son is going to be a sissy his entire life. Rather than kneel down and play with him, the father may yank the doll away and declare that boys don't do that sort of thing. The boy did nothing wrong in wanting to play with a doll rather than a toy gun; the dad's reaction was wrong.

If this small incident is one of many times of rejection when the father sees behavior he doesn't like or understand, alienation becomes a hallmark of the child's life from his early days. The father may withdraw from the son, leaving him to find male affection and acceptance from other sources.

If this son later finds that acceptance in the gay community, he will be convinced he was like all those other people from the time he was born. He'll be taught that if you're different, it must mean you're gay. And then this confused young man will be convinced that the only right thing to do is to sexualize the feelings and become involved in homosexual behavior.

At that point, he will find it difficult to believe he wasn't gay from birth. But he wasn't. He was just different, and that difference led to rejection by society and the father whose love he desperately needed.

Our mandate as parents is to love our children. The best thing we can do in this difficult area is to celebrate the special talents and uniqueness of each child. Even if our kids don't do all the things our culture says little boys and girls should do, we need to accept them as special, wonderful creations of God who crave our love and acceptance. This is our best hope of keeping them from seeking love in the wrong places.

Let's go from the abstract to a real example of the need to provide acceptance to children. Steve's brother, Jerry, who died as a result of AIDS in 1988, said that he felt different and had interests different from those of other boys even when he was very young. While they played with trucks, he preferred dolls. While they played army with toy guns, his "weapon" became a sewing machine with which he made doll clothes.

This did not fit the image of an ideal son for their rugged Texan father. In fact, Jerry's desire to do traditionally female activities caused their dad to distance himself from Jerry, and Jerry to pull away from their father. But by itself, this distancing didn't produce a homosexual child; Jerry didn't have a sexual experience with a man until he was in his twenties.

Before Jerry died, he revealed his feelings and experiences in his book, *How Will I Tell My Mother?* It provides keen insights into the development of homosexuality. Jerry never tried to justify what he had done or the gay lifestyle he lived. He said clearly that he had made a terrible mistake in going the way of the world rather than the way of God's choosing. But he also made it clear that his unique talents and personality traits had caused him to feel rejected by the culture and his father, leaving unmet his deep, natural need for male affection.

Jerry's need and desires were not wrong. The wrongness occurred when he eventually decided to sexualize the need and engage in homosexual behavior.

We must not accept the cultural bias regarding appropriate male and female traits in children, nor the validity of such terms as *tomboy, sissy, effeminate,* and *male pursuits*. For many involved in homosexual behavior, these terms and the cultural assumptions they carry bear more of the responsibility than we realize. The result is unhealthy alienation that drives children to find love and acceptance in the wrong places.

As parents, we must fight the urge to reject, label, and make false assumptions. We must encourage our kids to develop their talents. We must give up our preconceived images of what a "real boy" and "real girl" should be and simply love the boys and girls we have. This is our greatest hope of raising kids who make sexual choices in line with God's best for them. And we can never forget that our children will—must—find somewhere the love and acceptance they need every bit as much as they need food and water. If we don't provide it, someone else will.

You Can Make a Difference

Often in our youth groups, we have seen kids come in who we felt were on a track toward homosexuality. They were very sensitive, and their peers avoided them. The parents of these children were often distraught over what they could do to encourage more normal behavior and peer acceptance. Sometimes the parents were ashamed of their children and wanted to know if there was something they could do to reverse the direction these children were taking. The parents also wanted us to confirm whether their fears were realistic.

Although there are no easy solutions when children become confused about their sexual orientation, parents must consider four basic truths:

1. Not all boys who have effeminate characteristics or girls who have manly characteristics grow up to be gay. And not all homosexuals had such characteristics when they were children.

2. Parental actions don't guarantee change. Parents can do everything within their human power, and ask for God's help as well, but their children still have free will and are responsible for their decisions and actions.

3. No child is immune to temptation. No matter what we do to protect our children, there will probably come a time when they will be tempted to participate in exploration of their sexuality. For most, it's a passing event that has little or no impact on their lives.

   It's important that we don't overreact and inflict severe punishment for the children's behavior during this developmental stage. However, if we know homosexual behavior has occurred, we shouldn't send a message of approval. We should take the event as an opportunity to teach biblical standards of sexual behavior. That way, we will prick their consciences without traumatizing them.

It's vital that children know that one homosexual experimentation does not mean they're gay. Many in the gay community want children to believe that myth. They use it to encourage them to press further into the gay lifestyle.

4. Remember that in God's eyes, all sin is equal. All sin offends Him and affects our lives. Homosexual behavior is not a bigger sin than adultery. Often those who are guilty of other sins hold homosexuality up as the worst sin and place all those involved in it into a special class of sinner. But the homosexual is not beyond God's grace.

Preventive Steps

The parents' first step toward prevention of homosexuality is to recognize the early signs, or predictors, of a homosexual inclination within their child's behavior and personality. Parents can then respond by providing alternative activities and relationships while ensuring that the child feel unconditional love and acceptance.

Recognize Early Signs and the Greatest Predictors

Some characteristics are common to many homosexuals. If your children exhibit some of these traits, it does not mean they will enter a gay lifestyle, and overreacting and punishing will only create additional problems. Accepting and loving them will provide a greater chance for normal development, no matter what problems confront them. Some of the possible indicators are given here.

They dislike traditional games for their gender. In this pattern, a boy associates with more feminine pursuits and a girl with more masculine pursuits. However, in the area of male sports—basically rough, competitive, and physical activities—a boy may initially shy away simply for physiological reasons. Girls, on the other hand, may be attracted to rougher activities because they want to use their bodies, which may be considerably more developed than their friends'. Problems come when the parents can't accept the children's interests. That causes kids to become obsessed with obtaining approval from others, since they feel rejected by their parents.

If your son is slight of build for his age or near-sighted (affecting eye-hand coordination), he may withdraw from sports simply for fear of physical injury or because he feels incompetent. This may earn him a label like "sissy" that only compounds his problem of self-worth and acceptance. Or he simply may not like the competition and prefer milder forms of entertainment.

Your young daughter may be a foot taller than her peers and be attracted to sports in which height is an asset, such as volleyball or basketball. If you become afraid of those interests and overreact, you'll alienate her rather than encourage her to develop a talent.

Remember to give your children much moral

support and acceptance if they dislike traditional games for their gender. It's especially important that you don't express disapproval and ridicule. If you are or were a talented athlete, it's often hard to learn that you have knock-kneed, wall-eyed, uncoordinated children. But set aside your disappointment and build up their self-esteem in other areas, perhaps in individual or one-on-one sports like table tennis, swimming, running, tennis, golf, or track.

If your child is a boy, "male" pursuits such as board games, miniature golfing, camping, or building model airplanes could also be substituted for team sports. Likewise, if your daughter displays the coordination and strength of a skilled athlete, help her develop those skills. If you would have preferred a ballerina but got a track star, give up your ideas and become your daughter's biggest fan.

They relate more to children of the opposite sex. Alienation received from same-sex peers may be the sole reason some children associate with and cling to an opposite-sex peer group at a time when most children avoid opposite-sex relationships. If your children continually align with the opposite sex, it might be a sign of gender-identification problems.

In this situation, encourage them. Rather than scolding or belittling their actions, reinforce your son's maleness or your daughter's femaleness with statements of affirmation and, again, open displays of affection such as hugging. Proven words of affirmation include: "What a great son you are!" "I'm so proud to have a little boy like you." "You hit a home run! You deserve a great big hug!" "I couldn't be prouder to have you as my daughter." The combinations are almost limitless.

Recognize Unhealthy Family Traits and Behavioral Problems

The second step parents can take is to recognize unhealthy relationships and behavioral patterns within the family and change them into ones that will provide openness and communication. The law of cause and effect has not been repealed. If a child is experiencing alienation and isolation, the reason has to do with the way family members interact with that child.

Several family traits are common to many homosexuals' upbringing. Alienation, for example, seems to be the hallmark of a homosexual's early family life. Usually alienation takes shape through one of several family patterns.

The parents wanted a child of the opposite sex. A frequent comment among homosexuals is that their parents wanted a child of the opposite sex. This often happens when there's an older sibling of the same sex, and the parents wanted a child of the opposite gender to round out the family. Comments such as "You should have been a boy" or "You would have made a pretty girl" are devastating to a child.

Some parents who wanted a child of the opposite sex even cross-dress their sons and daughters. The underlying message to any intelligent or sensitive child is clear: To be accepted and win my parents' approval, I need to act, dress, and be something and someone I'm not. It's an enormous message of disapproval and rejection. At no time should such comments be made, nor should children ever be dressed in clothing that is obviously designed for the opposite sex.

If you've been making such statements, immediately apologize and reaffirm your child's place in the family. Here's an idea of what you might say: "Johnny, you know Mommy and Daddy used to say we wanted you to be a little girl when you were born. We want you to know that we are very sorry we said that, because we know you're the most perfect little boy for us. We are so happy to have a son like you! We're glad to have your big brother, Tom, and we're glad he can have you for a little brother. You are such a wonderful son for us!"

The father is absent, distant, or abusive. A weak father-child relationship is another common trait in most homosexuals' upbringing. They frequently comment that they never felt their fathers' approval. More bluntly, some male homosexuals describe their homosexual affairs as blatant attempts to obtain affection they never received from their fathers. A female with an abusive father, on the other hand, may seek a female relationship out of fear that all males will ultimately be abusive.

If there's no father in the family, the son nonetheless will need a male figure to model. The daughter also needs a male figure so she can learn to relate to males emotionally. The single parent should seek out a relative, become involved in a big-brother program, or approach the church for help.

Many churches have started programs in which college males or other men spend time with boys and girls who have no fathers. Of course, great caution must be taken. These programs could provide an opportunity for children to be abused. Before they enter a program like this, children need specific instructions on not allowing anyone to touch their genital area. If you can't have that kind of discussion with your kids, you need a counselor to help you.

Some important words are now in order for fathers who may not be living at home or have difficulty dealing with their emotions.

Fathers need to express affection for their sons and to show it in an open and honest way. Fathers should also be sure to find ways to relate to their daughters appropriately. They should ensure that their daughters don't come to fear men because of their fathers' insensitivity. As simple as this sounds, however, fathers often find they can't do this because of patterns in their own family background. If you feel this way, seriously consider working with a family counselor.

The inability to express love for a child is a tough issue from several perspectives, because men who have this difficulty are usually afraid of appearing to be "weak" by going to a counselor. Men, especially, need to be able to show emotions of concern and care, and to admit their weaknesses and inadequacies. It's difficult for children to forever measure up to a perfect father. It's far more important for them to see how a parent handles mistakes than to see no mistakes at all.

Frank Pittman, a psychiatrist and family therapist, puts this more succinctly. Describing the problem between fathers and sons, he said, "Fathers also have the job of telling their sons when the boy is masculine enough to be accepted as a man."[1] If a man defines masculinity in terms of athletic prowess, his son will never feel like a man unless he achieves in sports.

Pittman continues: "Men who don't feel masculine enough suffer from 'father hunger'—a gnawing need for a man, whether a grandfather, uncle, stepfather, or mentor—to welcome them into manhood. We need an older man to model more nurturing images of masculinity for us and to tell us we are lovable and acceptable to other men."

The child was molested. Molestation is a terrifying experience for any child. But sadder still is the aftermath in which parents who have developed patterns of emotional distance, avoidance, and nonconfrontation can never help their child heal and become whole.

In the example of Grant at the beginning of this chapter, we see three main themes. First, the "emotionally distant" father provided no bridge for communication, which is important in building a father-son bond.

Second, the mother didn't "tune in" and listen to what Grant said. A 10-year-old boy who states that an unknown male "hugged him differently" begs to be heard. Although children are often inarticulate, this sounds like something out of the ordinary.

Third, he was molested by an authority figure. He believed that since the man was important, what he was doing couldn't be wrong.

Parents need to work continually on opening lines of communication. No subject should be barred from parent-child discussion.

Teach your children at an early age that their bodies are the temples of the Holy Spirit and are to be treated with respect. Don't try to scare them unnecessarily about molestation. Simply explain that no one should be allowed to touch their bodies in the area a bathing suit would cover. Should anyone touch them in that area, train them to say, "Stop, you're not allowed to touch me," and run to another adult. It's right for children to tell parents or another adult anytime something or someone makes them "feel funny" or "mixed up."

Finally, be an active listener and communicator. There was probably no way Grant's parents could have expected the molestation to occur or even to have protected Grant from the adult's advances. But if they hadn't been too embarrassed to bring up the subject with Grant and to train him to defend himself, and if they had been active listeners and communicators, they could have helped Grant handle the aftermath in a way that enforced his feelings of self-esteem, acceptance, and wholeness.

Try also to keep your children in wholesome environments. The church can be that place, but never assume that all the people there are healthy. Don't easily entrust your children to someone else. Be careful when you turn your children over to anyone else's care.

Is There Ever Hope a Homosexual Will Change?

Secular wisdom insists that homosexuals should explore the facets of their sexual orientation and seek ways to be comfortable with—even proud of—their sexual identity. But if we parents know that homosexuality is not a natural lifestyle (and biblically we know that), such an approach provides no hope or comfort.

On the other hand, many men and women have been able to leave the homosexual lifestyle through the grace of God. Christians can take heart in knowing they "can do every thing through [Christ] who gives [us] strength" (Phil. 4:13). But forsaking homosexual behavior is never easy and never instant. It takes time and ongoing accountability with others who are holding fast to the biblical mandate. Like any other problem, this one can't be wished away.

If your children are already involved in homosexual behavior and starting to identify with the homosexual lifestyle, they need your love and acceptance—now more than ever. Parents often withhold these out of a fear that their children will think they condone homosexual behavior. Don't let the conflict move your children further from you. The relationship may be rough, but if you will persevere and be there for them, there is hope that they will once again walk free to become all that God wants for them.

In working with kids who became involved with homosexuality, we have counseled their parents to pray, be patient, and show their undying love. We have watched many parents rejoice because their sons and daughters have decided not to follow a homosexual lifestyle. There have been great victories and times of emotional healing in numerous families.

Don't give up on your children. Show God's relentless love by loving them relentlessly, even when it feels like the hardest thing in the world you could possibly do.

CHAPTER ELEVEN

AIDS

In the beginning of 1991, people were starting to forget that there was an AIDS epidemic. Many people thought it was going away. Some kids we spoke with were more sexually active than they'd been in previous years. The possibility of contracting AIDS didn't alter their lifestyles one bit. Then Magic Johnson shocked the world with the news that no one is immune. Even the most loved, most famous, and most unlikely people are candidates for AIDS.

Many families have had far more personal encounters with AIDS. One mother was horrified to learn that her daughter was pregnant. She was dealt another blow when she learned that the young man who had impregnated her daughter was HIV-infected and that her daughter had also acquired the virus. Shortly after the baby was born, it also tested

HIV-positive. Lives have been shattered, and the boy continues to have sex with any girl he meets. What a tragedy for this family, who experienced the reality and full impact of AIDS long before Magic Johnson admitted to being one of the worst moral role models in the history of sports.

Magic Johnson's admission that he was HIV-positive did two things. First, it reminded all of us just how many people are having sex outside of marriage. It's a way of life for many basketball and other sports heroes. For some of the kids we work with, ongoing sexual activity is also a way of life. Out of complete rebellion or a desire to fulfill unmet needs, kids are having sexual intercourse at younger ages and with more partners. Each time they do, they play Russian roulette with the AIDS virus.

Second, Magic Johnson's admission reinforced the fact that HIV, the virus that causes AIDS, can be contracted by anyone. If your daughter is sexually active, you may not only have a problem right now. You may also be in store for the heartache of your life, as the following illustration shows.

Felicia is pretty straight. At her California high school, she was a student leader and almost always on the honor role. Most of the time, she was involved in group activities and usually double-dated with her best friend. Although she was not active in any church, Felicia was a "good kid." She had nothing to do with the drug scene or alcohol.

At the end of Felicia's freshman year of high

school, a sophomore named Mark took a special interest in her. They seemed to share many traditional values: honesty, clean living, monogamous relationships, and wholesome activities. Although he had dabbled a bit in the drug scene, Mark had left that stage of rebellion behind him. As time went on, they became closer, not only socially and psychologically, but physically as well. When Felicia lost her virginity to Mark, he told her he had "been with only" two girls in high school.

During the next few years, many changes took place. Felicia moved to Minnesota, while Mark stayed in California. But they wrote and called each other often, and the relationship deepened despite the distance. After some time passed, they decided to attend the same college, where they continued to see each other. By September of Felicia's junior year in college, they began to talk about getting married after graduation.

Mark flew out at Thanksgiving to meet her parents. Everything went smoothly; her parents loved him. The rest of the school year sailed by, and Mark gave her a promise ring to carry her through the summer.

Mark's senior year was hectic but happy. He had a great life ahead. He planned to graduate, get a year's start in his career, and marry Felicia after her graduation. Felicia's junior year of college was exhausting, but Mark's support helped to carry her through. She stayed in California to work during the summer so she could be close to him.

By fall, Felicia found that "senioritis" was already taking its toll. She constantly felt fatigued, and by midafternoon each day she was utterly exhausted. When Felicia developed a bad chest cold that she couldn't shake after six weeks, her friends suggested she might have walking pneumonia. She made an appointment to see Dr. Lambert, the doctor at the school clinic. He ran a number of tests and suggested that she be hospitalized for a few days, while he ran more tests.

Although Felicia worried about missing school, she welcomed the idea of complete rest and recuperation and checked in on a Thursday. The second night in the hospital, she sensed something was wrong. When she questioned a pair of nurses who came to take care of her, they just looked at each other. Then one stated that Felicia's physician had suggested there might be a danger of infection and that he could tell her more about it the following morning.

"Your blood tests confirm you're infected with the AIDS virus," Dr. Lambert told her gently on Saturday morning.

Felicia gasped. "Oh no. That's a complete mistake. There's no way. There's positively no way. Doctor, I'm not a male homosexual! I'm straight. I've had only one sex partner, and we've both been faithful to each other. He's not gay, and we don't use drugs! This is absolutely impossible."

But Dr. Lambert's tests were conclusive, and Mark also tested HIV-positive. After taking a careful history, the doctor determined that while in high school, during one of the three times he had sampled "crystal meth"—an injectable drug—Mark had shared needles and syringes with other guys from the "drug den" and had contracted the AIDS virus when a minute amount of infected blood had been passed to his body.

Felicia is now 25 and dying of AIDS. Two others look as if they are dying: Felicia's parents. In a million years, they'd never have dreamed this fate was possible for Felicia. The fact that she is such a wonderful girl made living with the reality of AIDS that much more painful.

The news could not have hit Felicia's mother any harder. Devastated, she went into a deep depression. When her daughter needed her the most, she wasn't emotionally available. She has been hospitalized numerous times, continues to take antidepressant medication, and spends many of her waking hours in tears. For her, AIDS hit home much too hard.

Felicia's father feels that while AIDS is taking the life of his daughter, its emotional impact is taking the life of his wife. He never experienced such grief before. Some days, he's tempted to end the struggle for all of them. Other days, he just mumbles two words: "Why, God?"

A dark cloud entered the lives of this family—and Mark's family—the day Felicia was diagnosed with AIDS, and it lingers, stinging their eyes and ripping their hearts a little more every moment as they mourn the future loss of a daughter. Sadly, more and more parents of wonderful teenagers will experience the same devastation.

The Facts

The Centers for Disease Control in Atlanta, which compile statistics on diseases in the United States, report that since June 1981 there have been:

- an estimated 1.5 million people infected with the HIV virus, many of whom continue to have frequent sexual intercourse and exchange unclean needles. We can only imagine how many will be infected by the year 2000.
- two-hundred-six thousand cases of AIDS reported through February 1992. This is a confusing figure. To be classified as having AIDS, a person has to experience one of the opportunistic diseases that eventually kills him or her. Since it often takes about 10 years, and sometimes longer, for a person to go from being HIV-infected to having AIDS, the severity of the AIDS epidemic is sometimes overlooked. Unless some new drug or technology is developed, all of the 1.5 million HIV-infected individuals will eventually contract AIDS.
- as of February 1992, 136,000 deaths due to AIDS. The odds of dying from the AIDS virus are still 100 chances out of 100.
- thirty-six thousand cases of AIDS among young people ages 20 to 29.

There are fewer than 1,000 reported cases of AIDS among 13- to 19-year-olds, but that statistic jumps 10 times higher to more than 8,000 cases among 20- to 24-year-olds. Since AIDS symptoms take years to appear, this points to teenagers as being an at-risk group. Many health professionals fear that teenagers may possibly become the "third wave" of the AIDS epidemic in the United States, following gay men and intravenous drug users. Teens are most likely the fastest-growing group of HIV-infected people.

Methods of Transmission Among Teens

There are primarily two ways a teen or adult can acquire the Human Immunodeficiency Virus (HIV) that causes AIDS. It's transmitted almost entirely through either sexual intercourse (including anal intercourse) with an infected partner or by sharing intravenous needles or syringes that are infected with the virus from a previous user. Let's look at both methods in more detail.

Sex. Hugging, holding hands, or even kissing a person with AIDS are not methods of transmission. All transmission is linked to seminal, vaginal, or cervical body fluids or the exchange of blood and not saliva. If a person doesn't have sex with someone who has the AIDS virus or doesn't share a needle or syringe, his or her chance of becoming infected with HIV is less than being hit by a meteor. It's important to know this so that if you have an opportunity to minister to someone with HIV, you will not back away.

The most likely way for teenagers to acquire HIV is through sex. Despite admonitions to "just say no," the majority of teens in the United States have their first sexual experiences between the ages of 15 and 19; the average American teen loses his or her virginity by 16.

Most teenagers are aware of AIDS and its dangers, but the whole concept of its long-term impact is still beyond their comprehension. Although most young people know which behaviors are statistically risky, those same teens can't comprehend on the psychosocial level that they could become infected. They frequently think, *I won't get it; it'll never happen to me*. Rarely have we met a teenager who didn't feel invincible or immortal.

The closest teenagers have come to accepting the reality of AIDS was when Magic Johnson was found to be infected with HIV. That seemed to be a wake-up call to America's youth that no one is exempt from AIDS. The only problem is that Magic placed too much emphasis on the need for condoms and too little on the need for kids to abstain from sex altogether. He eventually came around to say that abstinence is the best way to avoid AIDS, but those statements were too little and too late to have much impact. When talking with Arsenio Hall on national television, he encouraged the use of condoms. But when he talked of abstinence, the news was reported somewhere other than the front page of most newspapers.

A recent study indicated that teens are far more worried about becoming pregnant than they are about getting AIDS. As great as teenagers' fear of pregnancy is, it does little to alter their behavior. Sexually active teens commonly engage in sexual activity for several years before obtaining birth-control pills to prevent pregnancy. This is why passing out condoms is such a misguided approach. Not only do they fail, but kids rarely use them to prevent either pregnancy or AIDS.

As parents, we must also teach our children that "safe sex" is a myth. Richard Keeling, M.D., chairman of the American College Health Association, states, "When you're impaired by alcohol, there is no such thing as safe sex."[1] Under the influence of alcohol, teens engage in far more risky behavior, such as unprotected sex and sex with multiple partners. Dr. Keeling failed to say that there's no such thing as "safe sex," even when a teenager isn't drinking. Condoms can't be relied on to prevent either pregnancy or sexually transmitted diseases. Condoms fail about 20 percent of the time when used by couples as a sole means of pregnancy prevention. Sex is never safe unless it's within the confines of marriage, as God has instituted.

Drug use. The second most common means of AIDS transmission is intravenous drug use. If you know or strongly suspect that your child is a drug user and you're waiting for him or her to grow out of that phase, you're making a terrible mistake. Those who use drugs—intravenous or otherwise—are sitting ducks for the AIDS virus. As cocaine use rises among teens, the rate of HIV infection among this group will most likely also rise. That's because the influence of alcohol and other drugs leads to promiscuity, and sex is often traded for drugs or used to acquire money to buy drugs that support addiction.

Do everything within your power to obtain professional treatment for your child if you suspect he or she is a drug user. In this day and age, parents who wait often must live with tremendous guilt because they didn't intervene sooner. Remember, if your child is involved with illicit drugs, he or she is beyond the ability to make a rational decision to change. The child will remain hooked until you—the parent—take drastic measures to stop the problem from progressing.

High school and college athletes often take steroids to increase athletic performance. A survey by the National College Athletic Association found that as many as 30 percent of male student athletes, who were involved in sports in which performance is enhanced through steroid use, exhibited evidence of the drug. Sharing needles and syringes as a means to inject steroids has great potential for AIDS transmission.

Which Teens Face the Greatest Risk?

Dr. Mary-Ann Shafer suggests that four teen groups are at risk for HIV infection:

1. The youngster who experiments early with cigarettes, alcohol, sex, and drugs could be in danger. The child who tries a cigarette in the fourth or fifth grade will likely engage in riskier behavior later.

2. Girls who develop physically at an early age. The girl who looks like she's 20 when she's only 12 could be at risk because she may unwittingly attract older men, yet she lacks the maturity or social skills to protect herself from unwelcome advances or other pressure situations.

3. Teens who have serious problems at school are at risk because they probably lack self-esteem and are likely to be tempted by drugs, alcohol, or sex in order to feel good about themselves.

4. Impoverished teens in inner cities are in a special-risk category because, more than likely, tremendous drug activity takes place in their neighborhoods, and there's far more peer pressure to deal drugs (which usually ends in drug abuse), use drugs, and have sex at an early age.[2]

You Can Make a Difference

There has never been a more serious problem accompanied by greater parental denial than HIV infection and AIDS. Most parents simply can't imagine the possibility of their children becoming ill with this disease because it leads to such a horrible fate. Yet more and more parents are having to wake up to the horror of losing children to this killer virus. The HIV-infected population is growing larger, not smaller. More people will be infected this year than last. The chances are increasing that your child will be exposed to this virus if he or she is sexually active or an intravenous drug user. However, you don't have to sit back and hope for the best or even expect the worst. You can and need to take preventive steps.

Talk to Your Kids

Ask your children what they know about AIDS. Ask them what the truth about AIDS means to them personally. Tell them about the reality of this disease. Don't expect anyone else to do it for you. Let them know you're an accurate source of knowledge. If you aren't, call an AIDS hot line and order literature so you can win the battle for credibility with your children.

Be Willing to Intervene

If you know your child is participating in risky sexual behaviors, intervene before it's too late. If possible, sit down with other sets of parents and make the tough decisions about protection. Determine the hours when the children can be together and where they're allowed to go when they're together. Enter into an educational process with those parents, with the goal of helping the kids recognize the physical, emotional, and spiritual consequences of continuing to have sex so they will decide to abstain. The most important thing is to communicate that you expect abstinence and that you will ask your child about his or her sexual behavior in the future. Emphasize that the goal is for him or her to be able to look you in the eye and say, "I have decided to wait."

If your child uses drugs, especially intravenously, obtain treatment as soon as possible. Home remedies don't solve this problem. To wait may be to wait too long. Your goal is to help the child eliminate the high-risk behavior as soon as possible.

What to Do If AIDS Comes Home

The best advice we can give parents of a child with AIDS is to listen to someone who has been there. Jerry Arterburn's book *How Will I Tell My Mother?* was written just months before he died of AIDS and offers this simple, straightforward advice for the parents of young people who have contracted AIDS:

> Don't spend the rest of your life with the guilt of knowing that when your child needed you the most, you didn't help. You may need professional counseling to help you make it through this difficult experience. Whatever it takes, for your sake and that of your child, obtain the help you need. . . .
>
> When I went for treatment at the Institute for Immunological Disorders in Houston, I (saw) hundreds of people with AIDS who had been abandoned by their families. Not only had they been abandoned, but they had also been literally cast out of their families. They would lie in their room for days with no visitors. Their families couldn't cope with the reality of what happens in an imperfect world.

If your child has the disease called AIDS, I beg of you to do what Christ has asked you to do, and that is to love him or her. If you don't, your rejection will intensify the guilt and condemnation that he or she already feels. Please dig deep in your heart and find that love.[3]

A Personal Note from Steve

My family was just like all the rest. We thought AIDS was a problem other people had to deal with. We never dreamed we'd have someone with AIDS in our family. What a shock for me to learn that the brother I had respected the most and wanted to be like the most was dying from AIDS! My shock was mild, though, compared to that of my parents. There's no way you can imagine the depth of their pain without actually seeing their faces. It was a tragedy they were not prepared to handle. But through the power and comfort of the Holy Spirit, they handled it. They showed love to my brother right up until June 13, 1988, when he died. I've never been more proud of my parents than while watching them go beyond their limits to show love to their hurting son.

Having lived through this experience, I want to appeal to you on a personal level to do everything within your power to prevent this from happening to one of your children. Begin a family counseling process if conflicts are leading a teenager to be rebellious. Obtain help for your child if there's a drinking or drug problem. Monitor who your son or daughter dates and spends time with. Don't be intimidated by a teenager. Don't be manipulated into allowing your child to be with someone you believe is an unhealthy influence.

The value of a child's life can't be measured. Yet the AIDS virus is a deadly destroyer of so many precious lives that have such great potential. Every uncomfortable moment you spend preventing AIDS from hurting your child—or other children—will be more than worth the discomfort.

CHAPTER TWELVE

Pornography

We have both been working in various aspects of ministry for more than 15 years, so very little shocks either of us. But during the past several years, we have been a bit shocked by the revelations of some people in Christian ministry who have secretly used pornography. In nearly every case we've dealt with, the use of pornography began when the people were adolescents. If children make it out of adolescence without being heavily exposed to pornography, they most likely won't develop a problem with it later on. But in today's culture, few people are able to live without some form of pornography being thrust upon them. Even if they grow up to become ministers, the chances are great that the pornographic shadow will continue to hover around them.

For example, while attending an Atlanta conference for youth workers last summer, we were amazed by the number of young men who wanted to talk to us about their problems with pornography. Several men had been lured in by the Wildcat Lounge just across the freeway from the hotel. One man told us that he had seen it on the way in and was determined to stay away. But in the middle of the night, he was compelled to go there and see the nude dancers. Magazines and videos no longer satisfied him; he wanted to see real people. He couldn't believe that he had come to Atlanta to become a better minister, yet he could not stay out of a strip joint. Ironically, he was shocked to find other youth ministers there. His story, like almost every other one we've heard, began with an interest in pornography at an early age.

Another youth minister revealed that his fascination with pornography had begun at age 11, when his brothers exposed him to lewd material. Ever since, he had developed a private world that he couldn't avoid. It had led to compulsive masturbation that he'd hoped would stop once he was married, but it hadn't. Riddled with guilt and shame, he enjoyed sex more alone than with his wonderful wife.

We are convinced that these stories aren't rare. Since we talk about pornography and sexual addiction, people naturally feel able to talk to us about it. But we believe thousands of others never talk to anyone. They are as hooked on pornography as a heroin addict is on heroin.[1] The only difference is that their shame is much greater. If we parents are to prevent future generations from experiencing lives of guilt and shame due to pornography, we must stop their exposure to pornography during their growing-up years.

Not all the people who become hooked on pornography fit the profile of a minister who harbors a dark secret. Almost everyone has heard of Ted Bundy, the serial killer who was responsible for the deaths of at least 28 women and children. He dramatically illustrates how someone can be victimized by pornography. In his case, pornography so enveloped his identity that it robbed him of his freedom and eventually took his life. Who knows what Ted Bundy would have been like if he hadn't been exposed to pornography in his early teen years?

Not everyone is aware that just hours before he was executed, Ted Bundy spoke to Dr. James Dobson, a noted Christian psychologist and head of Focus on the Family. Not only did Bundy confess his guilt and responsibility for the murders, but he also provided an unusual "exposé" of the role pornography had played in his life. He explained:

> Basically, I was a normal person. I wasn't someone you'd look at and say, "There's a pervert." I had good friends. I led a normal life—except one small but very potent and destructive segment of it that I kept secret and very close to myself and didn't let anybody know about.
>
> I don't know why I was so vulnerable to it. All I know is pornography had an impact on

me that was central to the development of the violent behavior that I engaged in.

I look at pornography as an addiction. You keep craving something that is harder and harder, which gives you a greater sense of excitement, until you reach a point where pornography only goes so far. You reach that jumping-off point where you begin to wonder if actually doing it will give you that which is beyond just reading about it or looking at it.

Pornography can reach out and snatch any kid out of any house today.

The most damaging kinds of pornography, and I am talking from hard, real, personal experience, are those that involve violence and sexual violence. The wedding of those two forces, as I know only too well, brings behavior that is just too terrible to discuss.

There are those loose in towns and communities today, people like me, whose dangerous impulses are being fueled day in and out by violence in the media in its various forms, particularly sexualized violence.

There are forces loose in the country, particularly against this kind of violent pornography, where, on the one hand, well-meaning, decent people will condemn the behavior of a Ted Bundy while they are walking past a magazine rack full of the very kinds of things that [lead] young kids down the road to being Ted Bundy. That's the irony.

I've lived in prison a long time now. I've met a lot of men who were motivated to commit violence just like me, and without exception every one of them was deeply involved in pornography; without question, deeply influenced and consumed by an addiction to pornography. There's no question about it.[2]

Ted Bundy is a grim reminder that the gateway to sexual addiction, and sometimes sexual violence and murder, is pornography. The fathers who go to the local video stores and rent X-rated videos may never murder people as Ted Bundy did. But they have something in common with him. They're trapped and often don't know it. They certainly don't know how to get out. And most important, the bond they share is that their problem, though less severe, is no less painful.

Colleen Applegate presents another side of the pornography tragedy and the victimization it causes.

Shattered Innocence, a CBS television movie that aired a few years ago, highlighted her true story. The eldest of five children, Colleen was an easygoing kid from a nice, respectable midwestern family. Her father held a good managerial position with the telephone company, and her concerned mother was a devoted wife. On the other hand, a pervasive atmosphere of emotional distancing, a rigid discipline style, and an inability to express feelings dominated this "good" family.

The emotional distancing may have affected Colleen the most. Although she had always been a clean-cut, reasonable kid, Colleen "went off the deep end" while a senior in high school. She became involved with an older boy, began drinking, and moved with a wilder crowd. Shortly after graduation, she attempted suicide. The family entered counseling, but there was little confrontation about the family's communication problems.

Always a dreamer, Colleen and her boyfriend went to California a year later. There she found work as a "model," as she told her parents, for $100 a day. In fact, she was posing in the nude for skin magazines. Her parents learned the truth and insisted that she get out of the business, but by then she was a confirmed star of *Penthouse* and *Hustler*.

Barely six months later, Colleen graduated to porn films and was spotted by Buddy Hollander, a porn-film king. By the next year, she was earning more than $100,000, was featured having on-screen sex with nearly 40 different men, had contracted herpes, had had an abortion, and had developed a raging cocaine habit that consumed most of her income.

Colleen would have broken any mother's heart. By mid-1983, Colleen told her family that she was going to quit nude modeling. Her parents knew about the skin magazines but had no idea about the movies. Through Buddy Hollander, Colleen had met a new boyfriend who was more than twice her age. Her new beau was a coke dealer and kept Colleen fully supplied. When he was picked up on a drug charge in February 1984, she became depressed and spent most of his money on more cocaine.

The following month, Colleen attended the porn-film awards ceremony, where she received a generous offer to make another film. Running short on cash, she accepted. She was as hooked on the industry as many of the men were on the pictures she provided. But she never made that next film. A week later, Colleen picked up her boyfriend's semiautomatic rifle and shot herself through the head.

It would be very hard to convince Colleen's parents that hard-core pornography is not a crime and especially that it claims no victims.

Randy Oliver, age 14, is yet another reminder of how quickly pornography can engulf a person. He came into treatment after a referral from a local physician. In agony and shame, Randy's parents had taken him to the doctor after they found him masturbating in his bedroom, a magazine at his side and blood on his bed. It wasn't the first time that blood had been there, but Randy had convinced his mother that it came from a cut on his leg. Now his parents knew the real source. Randy was so compulsive in his masturbation that he couldn't stop, even though his penis was covered with sores.

The physician had dealt with problems like this before, but never with such a young boy. The problem had gone far beyond what most would characterize as normal adolescent sexual exploration.

Randy was a sex addict who couldn't control his masturbation. He was as hooked on pornography as anyone could possibly get. The combination of pornography and masturbation had become his "drug of choice" that he used as often as he could. A growing sense of shame infected every area of his personality.

The Private Lives of Men

This type of sexual addiction doesn't grip many young girls. Females are more frequently romantically and relationally addicted. Although sexual addiction is on the rise among females, it is mostly a male problem that starts in adolescence when adults are more than willing to tell boys that what they're doing is normal even when the boys have no real knowledge of what they're doing. Based on our experience, we believe this problem has trapped more young men, and haunted them throughout their lives, than any other problem written about in this book. These men are not all sex addicts, but all of them have become accustomed to the world of pornographic fantasy and seek it out as often as they can. Eventually it ruins their relationship with God, their feelings of self-worth, and often their marriages. If their marriages do stay together, they are void of true intimacy because of the fantasies that exist in the men's minds. They may be there in body, but their minds are with others who in a different way have been victimized by the pornographic industry.

What Constitutes Pornography?

The word *pornography* comes from the Greek word *pornographos*, which refers to "writing out" the trade of the harlots. *Webster's* defines pornography as "the depiction of erotic behavior (as in pictures or writing) intended to cause sexual excitement." We parents tend to think of pornography as nude pictures, but it is more than that. Webster's definition encompasses romance novels whose main intent is to cause sexual excitement. Many soap operas also fit that definition. Women, who often have a hard time understanding how men can get hooked on nude pictures, better understand how romance novels and soap operas can control people's lives, sapping the intimacy from their relationships.

Unfortunately, the United States Supreme Court had a little more trouble than Webster's in legally defining the subject. In 1965, the Supreme Court provided a three-part test to determine obscenity (the legal term used for pornography):

a. The material must be "patently offensive."
b. It must appeal to "prurient interests."
c. It must have "no redeeming social value."

You can see that the court was trying to define hard-core pornography, not all pornography. Since each of the Supreme Court's tests uses terminology that is ambiguous and inexact, pornographers won another round in 1973, when Justice Warren Berger declared that material not having serious literary, artistic, political, or scientific value could be deemed obscene. The term *patently offensive* was clarified to mean:

a. Patently offensive representations or descriptions of ultimate sex acts, normal, perverted, actual, or simulated.

b. Patently offensive representations or descriptions of masturbation, excretory function, and lewd exhibition of the genitals.

Finally, the ruling provided that "one national standard" didn't exist. Rather, material could be judged according to the values of the state, city, or community in which the material exists. The rationale for this was that the standards of the people living in Las Vegas might be entirely different from those of people living in a small town in the Bible Belt.

Nonetheless, the law still provides sufficient ambiguity for many writers and artists to claim their rights under the First Amendment. Perhaps Supreme Court Justice Potter Stewart spoke for most concerned parents in America when he explained that although he couldn't define pornography, "I know it when I see it."

Gateway to Sexual Addiction

In a real and practical sense, pornography is fantasy; fantasy and pornography are closely related links in the sexual-addiction chain. Pornography is an industry based on fantasy, masturbation, and the use of erotic sounds and sights. The *Playboy* empire was built from money paid by men who wanted to masturbate with fantasy women. As they fantasized about airbrushed examples of perfection, many of these men left behind their marriages and the ability to become intimate with real human beings. Here are some of the fantasies that can readily be found in today's pornography:

- having sex with a small child
- having sex while inflicting pain on another
- using sex as an act of violence
- forcing sex on people and discovering that they enjoy it
- having sex with multiple partners at the same time

Pornography is sold as an emotional getaway car, a vehicle for those who want to escape. It takes people beyond the boundaries of their unlimited imaginations. When their wells of fantasy run dry, the porn industry is ready with a virtually endless supply of books, magazines, videos, telephone sex, and computer on-line images to help generate new fantasies. Pornography is a tool for going beyond reality, beyond the fantasy world of one's imagination. Once used, it's difficult to live without.

Facts About Pornography
It's Big Business

Pornography is now considered to be a $10 billion-a-year business in America. As far back as 1985, *Ladies Home Journal* gave an excellent exposé of the extent of the obscenity industry.

- Americans were spending $8 to $10 billion a year on pornography material. (That's more than the $6.2 billion grossed by all three major networks—ABC, NBC, CBS—combined.)
- More than 20 million Americans buy sexually oriented magazines every month.
- Fifteen percent of all videos sold in the U.S. are sexually explicit.

New Sources of Pornography

Every civilization has had some type of pornography—erotic material that was used for sexual stimulation. Today, new sources of pornography are being piped into our homes via computer on-line services, as well as the R- and X-rated movies shown on many cable systems.

900 Numbers

Several years ago, the telephone company introduced 900 numbers as a way people could make phone calls for an advertised fee per minute. The most controversial of these were dial-a-porn numbers. Callers could dial advertised 900 numbers and listen to conversations ranging from teasing, giggling girls reciting their favorite sexual fantasies to explicit sounds and commentary about actual sex acts, bestiality, child sex, and rape. The calls are automatically charged to the callers' numbers, with costs ranging from a little more than a dollar to more than $5 per minute. Many parents have been outraged to discover excessive phone bills run up by teenagers who tried dial-a-porn numbers out of curiosity and became hooked on the experience.

New Life Clinics have a special treatment program for sex addicts. Most of those who enter treatment for sexual addiction have spent large sums of money on telephone sex, masturbating while erotic things are said on a tape or by a live person on the other end of the line. It's not uncommon to hear stories of those who have spent more than a thousand dollars a month to fuel their habits. Some seek treatment after the telephone bill arrives and their wives discover the outrageous sum that is owed. Telephone companies and the FCC have received thousands of complaints because for a long time there was no way to stop children from making those calls and hearing pornography over the family phone. This seductive and secret form of stimulation has ensnared millions since its inception. It's another example of how saturated with sick sex our society has become.

Although most phone companies now provide a blocking system (in which parents must pay to block calls going to 900 numbers), it doesn't prevent a curious youth from going to a friend's house where the numbers aren't prohibited. Some of these young people become addicted and require counseling and treatment to overcome the effects of the X-rated conversations. U.S. Attorney Brent Ward was quoted as saying that many, if not most, of the 2.8 million callers to the dial-a-porn companies are minors aged 10 to 16. The problem received nationwide attention in 1987 when a 12-year-old boy molested a 4-year-old girl after listening to two hours of pornographic phone talk.

Computer Porn

Personal computers hooked up to modems can now receive erotic pictures, dirty jokes, and sexual messages, and—through the miracle of modern technology—animated nudes on the terminal screen.

Some parents would think this is harmless, but it's often more graphic than what is filmed in real life. Some of the language is shocking. What's more, the graphic pictures and text can often be downloaded and printed out on your computer printer. If your computer is hooked up to a modem, be sure to check which services have been used in the last month. You may discover that a lot of time is being spent on computer porn rather than on accessing the local library.

The Music Industry: Rock Bands, Lyrics, Videos, and Concerts

In our work with kids, we still find it hard to believe what an incredible influence the music industry has on children. Parents who don't monitor what music their children listen to and/or watch on MTV are neglecting a much-needed responsibility. Good kids have been weaned away from their families' Christian values due to the desire to look like and be like the MTV stars.

Rock 'n' roll has come a long way since the

suggestive pelvic thrusts of Elvis Presley some 30 years ago. In the mid-'70s, the Rolling Stones shocked feminists when their newest album was promoted on billboards that showed a bound, bruised, and beaten woman with the caption, "I'm Black and Blue from the Rolling Stones—and I Love It!"

Today's hard-rock bands often have lyrics that go beyond just "titillating" or "sexually suggestive." Not only are the lyrics explicitly obscene, but the rock concerts also leave little to the imagination, staging acts that show women being brutalized and raped on stage while teenage audiences scream and cheer their approval.

Concerned parents might be well advised to take a closer look at MTV. They are often stunned at how suggestive the videos are, but they forget that those are the milder video versions approved for television.

Those who have been brought up in the church have seen the tremendous impact music can have on people's lives. Many have made decisions to live for Christ because the gospel message came through a song. The spoken word can't pierce the heart like the gospel combined with music. If the power of music can be so positive, we must understand that the reverse can also be true. The negative, evil, cynical, and sexually suggestive messages of music are getting through to our kids because they're combined with graphic pictures. Some of those messages are powerful because they are delivered through socially acceptable pornography that is passed off as art.

Who Buys Pornography?

The United States Advisory Board for Social Concerns shows that minors read 70 percent of all pornographic magazines. Further estimates indicate that most hard-core porn viewers are males under age 20.[3] To a large extent, our young people are financing this entire industry. Adults who seek treatment for pornography addiction almost always refer back to the days when they were young and exposed to pornography. Regardless of whether these adults are involved in multiple affairs, compulsive masturbation, or nonstop use of prostitutes, they usually tell the same story about getting started with what seemed to be a harmless magazine containing nude photographs.

If you have a teenager, he or she is a target for the pornography industry. You should be aware of secretive behavior that goes beyond what would be expected from an adolescent. One magazine or photograph could be the tip of an iceberg-size stash of material that has captured your child. Whatever evidence you discover—a phone bill, a book, a magazine, a video—don't take the child's word that it was a one-time experience. Believe that the child is ashamed and trying to hide reality from you. If you ignore the evidence, you may be ignoring your child's subconscious attempt to get help. Be aware that an adolescent caught up in this problem is usually much too ashamed to ask for help.

You Can Make a Difference

1. If you've not discussed pornographic 900 numbers with your children, it would be wise to do so. If they are 12 or older, they may have been introduced to this medium by a friend. They need to know that you are aware of 900 numbers and that you are also aware of the dangers. Let them know that it's a curious game that can cost innocent kids much more than an expensive phone bill. Give examples of how people can waste thousands of dollars and hurt others from the use of the numbers. Help your children understand that the people on the other end are doing something they often hate to do but have resorted to out of desperation. Help your children see the value in avoiding anything that produces shame and must be covered up. Call your local phone company and find out what their policy is on 900 numbers and how you can remove the access to porn-call numbers from your line. We recommend that access to these numbers be denied from your home phone.

2. The U.S. Postal Service has two forms you can use to protect your home from unwanted pornographic material; they take effect in about one month. Form 2201 puts your name on a list not to receive sexually explicit materials. The other, form 2150, is used to stop a particular company from sending you advertisements, catalogs, or brochures that you find

offensive. (For instance, most parents will want to discontinue all intimate-apparel catalogs that young males use as soft porn.)

3. The Parents Music Resource Center reviews CDs for objectionable material and then works to have the records labeled if they contain such language. Monitor what your children listen to. Their music should not be off-limits for you. If their music is offensive, hold a conference with them and tell them the rules are changing. Tell them they will not be allowed to play this music anymore. Confiscate objectionable records, but pay them for every record you take. Tell them that from then on you will destroy any unacceptable record that comes into the house whether it be theirs or a friend's. If investigation reveals that your children are having a problem in this area, make a policy that within the first week of their acquiring it, you must listen to any new record.

4. Never rent a sexually explicit video. Let your children know from your example that your standards are high and that erotic material won't be tolerated. This is one area in which many parents compromise. Let children know that the nude body is nothing to be ashamed of, but it is to be shared only with the person to whom you are married.

5. Ask your children if they have ever been exposed to pornography, and discuss with them the victimization and exploitation that

accompanies it. Explain the biblical principle of sins of the heart being just as serious as sins carried out with the body.

6. Teach children to respect their bodies and the bodies of others. Be the adult who provides them with appropriate sex education, including a discussion about pornography.[4]

7. Discuss masturbation with your children. With rock stars like Madonna and Michael Jackson grabbing their crotches and simulating masturbation, you can be sure that children are discussing it. Be sure they know what a compulsive masturbator is and how easy it is to become trapped in the use of pornography.

8. If your child has a problem, seek help immediately. Don't rely on home remedies or harsh discipline. The problem is tough, and you'll need all the help you can get to overcome it.

In a *Christianity Today* editorial, Kenneth Kantzer suggested four steps for parents:

a. Teach sex education at home and in church-sponsored programs.

b. Speak out against pornography, whether to PTA groups or to family stores that sell those materials.

c. Support those who are waging a battle against porn through petitions, letters, and boycotts.

d. Support and encourage any forums that will help people distinguish between

opposition to pornography and the limita-
tions of free speech.[5]

9. We think it's important for you to consider
    calling the parents of the friends your child
    spends a considerable amount of time with to
    ensure that they feel the same way you do
    about all forms of pornography. It wouldn't
    be too much trouble to ensure that the parents
    of your child's good friends agree with your
    views on pornography and that they allow no
    pornographic material in their homes. Some
    of the parents of your child's friends may
    resent this, but your child is more important
    than those parents' attitudes and feelings.

The days are over when pornography was
confined to a dark section of town at X-rated movie
theaters. Pornography is distributed through the
phone, the television cable, bookstores, drugstores,
and local video stores. Its availability has given it a
new degree of acceptance in society. As parents, we
must counter this influence with love, example, and
instruction. Otherwise someone else will teach our
children about pornography, and the visual aids they
use may be so enticing that they lure our children into
a fantasy world full of guilt, shame, and remorse.

CHAPTER THIRTEEN

Runaways

Have you ever been to Hollywood? Have you ever wanted to live in a mansion near the movie stars? Perhaps you'd be walking down the street one evening beneath the lights in the midst of the glamour and come up beside Warren Beatty or Julia Roberts. Maybe they'd take a look at you and ask you to come to their house for dinner—or even to live with them. Perhaps they'd try to get you a part in a movie. Have you ever been so miserable that anything seems better than home, and Hollywood—especially the Hollywood that exists in the mind of a teenager— seems like paradise?

Perhaps you can't relate to those thoughts and dreams, but thousands of teenagers can. They long for a Hollywood that doesn't exist anywhere except in their minds. And if they are pushed hard enough, they will leave their homes and try to find this place that is, in reality, the furthest place from their dreams.

Hollywood isn't the only place kids run to, but it's one of the most popular. If you go there, you'll see some of the kids who make the trip. We live about an hour away from the Hollywood that destroys kids. The kids aren't hard to find. All you have to do is drive by. Most of them live on the streets almost all night, looking to turn a trick for lunch money or to feed a quickly developed drug habit. They live out a nightmare rather than the dream they longed for. Many of them will die. A few will find legitimate jobs. Some will go back home, but they never go back the same. They're always different, most of the time feeling more hopeless than when they left.

Doreen is an example of what happens to a runaway. Sitting at police headquarters, she didn't look 13. Like most runaways, she had already been sexually abused before leaving home and had just been picked up for prostitution. The dirt under her fingernails revealed some of the filth in which she lived. The track marks on her bruised but otherwise snow-white arms showed that drugs had already become part of her lifestyle. Her face was full of fear and anger, but if you looked close enough, you could see her desire to be loved and accepted by someone. As police officers pleaded with her to let them help her get back home, she talked about her journey to the land of runaway street kids.

"My father was a doper and an abuser," she

explained. "He sexually abused me and used me starting on my eighth birthday. My eighth birthday . . . that's
only second grade! I decided I couldn't take it anymore.
There was no one I could trust, no one I could talk to
. . . so I decided to run away. I had some idea the
streets weren't exactly safe, but at least I'd have a 50-
50 chance out there. I had no chance at home."

Doreen's chances on the street were less than 50-
50. She hadn't been in Hollywood two weeks before
she was hooked up with a pimp and began prostitut-
ing herself on the streets. Now she's tough and
refuses to admit the hurt she feels from the treatment
she has received from her parents and her current
occupation. The chances of her leaving the
Hollywood streets are slim. Once Hollywood — and
similar spots in cities across America — has young
girls down in its bowels, it seldom spits them out.
The people who make their living on the streets use
up the Doreens before they throw them away.

Then there was Robert. He decided to leave home
at 16 and headed for the streets of Hollywood. It was
a spur-of-the-moment decision, brought on when his
dad exploded after Robert walked through the front
door two hours after his curfew. "You're grounded,
young man! This is the fifth time this month, Rob!
And you can just forget about using the car the rest of
this summer. Go to your room and get ready for the
whipping of your life."

Robert was very angry. His dad hadn't even both-
ered to find out why he was late! He might have had a

good reason. *At any rate,* he thought, *it doesn't matter now.* He grabbed clothes to stuff into his gym bag. *I'll show my dad. I'll never come home. Boy, will he be sorry!*

Robert hitchhiked to Hollywood, just two hours away. The first day he wandered through the city, taking in the sights and relishing his grown-up liberty and independence. But that night, reality set in. Winter nights in Los Angeles can be cool. As the temperature dropped, Robert realized he didn't have enough money for a hotel. He slept under a bench in the park, using his clothes as both a blanket and pillow. Now he was scared.

The next morning he was hungry and bought a large bag of corn chips for breakfast. Then he wandered into a bus station to sit in the warmth and eat. An overweight, middle-aged man stood smoking a cigar in the corner of the lobby and eyed Rob carefully. Finally, he sauntered over.

"I've been watching you," the man said. "I'm sure others have told you that you are good-looking enough to be in pictures. I'd like to make that happen. Come with me and we'll talk about your future."

Before looking further at Rob's journey, let's gain some perspective on the problems of runaway children.

The Facts

Authorities estimate that at least one million teenagers in the United States—possibly as many as two million—run away each year. The figures are difficult to substantiate because so many runaways go unreported. Parents don't report the runaways because either they feel guilty that the child has run away or, in some cases, they encouraged the child to leave. Statistics from the United States Department of Health and Human Services indicate that 1,250,000 young people are classified as homeless runaways each year.

The recorded number of runaway, throwaway, and homeless kids aged 18 and under is at least 1,300,000 a year and rising.[1] Obviously, the problem isn't getting any better. What the statistics never reveal is the deep pain in the hearts of family members the runaways leave behind. The devastation parents feel is unbearable when they become aware of the dangers on the streets and don't know where their children are sleeping. This pain is no greater than for a mother whose daughter left home after being sexually molested. *I could have done something to stop the abuse*, the mother thinks over and over. But it's too late.

More and more mothers and fathers are facing great pain because their children have become runaways. Some researchers believe the problem is a result of financial stress, which causes greater problems in homes. Other researchers believe that a lack of values taught early to children makes parents optional commodities in the minds of troubled children. Whatever the reasons, the problem is getting worse.

Runaways, by definition, are breaking the law by

leaving home before they turn 18. The lifestyle they adopt in order to survive will almost always involve additional illegal activities, especially prostitution and the use and sale of drugs. Rarely do runaways make it off the streets without embracing crime or contracting a disease that will stay with them for a lifetime or cut their lifetimes short.

Spiritual laws are also being broken when children leave home early. Breaking the laws of the land is less significant, in some respects, than breaking the laws of God. The rebellion of runaways becomes so strong that the outcome is often total self-destruction. God has given parents authority over children. Parental influence was established to provide children with a certain level of protection, even in dysfunctional homes, that is totally absent on the street. Runaway children enter an upside-down world where God doesn't matter. Only survival matters. Out of desperation, runaway children will do almost anything.

Defiant runaways are some of the loneliest and most pained children in the world. Their homes, or the homes they have created in their minds, must be horrific for them to not return to them after a few nights on the street. Because of the dangers on the street, runaways need our help perhaps more than any other group. We need to do whatever we can to reach them while there's still time.

Where Do Runaways Come From?

Runaways, who come from dysfunctional homes, are graphic evidence that families have failed to meet their emotional needs. They are evidence that parents—or others familiar with the situation—waited too long before making necessary changes. Most runaways come from abusive homes. Four years ago, the National Network of Runaway and Youth Services surveyed young people being helped in runaway shelters nationwide. Nearly two-thirds of those teenagers came from homes where they had been subjected to physical or sexual abuse.[2] There are no stereotypical runaways. They come from poor homes and from upper-middle-class homes. Although their demographics and psychographics may not be the same, one thread is common to all runaways: they all believe that the problems at home can't be resolved. Whether the problems are abuse—physical, emotional, or sexual—or disruptive situations such as serious illness or divorce, the runaways believe they have a better chance of survival outside their families than within them.

The development of this problem is complex. Often it begins when a young woman gets pregnant and raises the baby with little or no support from others. Twenty-five percent of runaways are born to mothers under age 18.[3] These teenage mothers often find themselves in situations where they become high school dropouts, have no job skills, and have an unstable living environment. This combination of poverty and lack of positive influence often drives children to try to make it apart from their families.

Leslie Morgan reported in *Seventeen* magazine:

> (The) profile of the average runaway varies
> from place to place. In New York, 65 percent
> are boys; 60 percent are Hispanics, and 10
> percent are white; the drug of choice is crack,
> and 7 percent test positive for AIDS.
>
> In Toronto, 80 percent of runaways are
> from middle- and upper-middle-income fami-
> lies and are white; 90 percent left home
> because they were sexually abused by some-
> one in their family, and cocaine is the favored
> drug.
>
> In Fort Lauderdale, the majority of
> runaways have been on their own since age
> 15; 5 percent are under age 6, and 90 percent
> have had some experience with prostitution,
> pornography, or both.[4]

These statistics bring us back to Robert's runaway
journey. The man took Robert to breakfast and
offered him a part in a movie. "If you go with me,"
the man said, "I will introduce you to a movie
producer, and they'll begin filming tonight." Robert
thought it was too good to be true, but people had
often told him he was handsome enough to be in
movies. So he went with the man and indeed met a
movie producer.

The producer told Robert that the only hitch to his
getting a contract was that he'd have to appear nude
and have sex with women while being filmed. To

Robert, this was quite a shock. He decided the best thing he could do was to get out of the place as soon as he could. He asked if he could think about it, and they said he could. He left with their phone number but never intended to use it.

It took only four more days of struggling on the streets before Robert called the people back and told them he was ready to make a movie. For $1,000 he had sex with a woman three times his age while being filmed. Although his actions disgusted him greatly and he vowed never to do it again, he was hooked. When the $1,000 was gone, he was back in the movie business again.

That's how Robert got lost in the seamy side of Hollywood. Before his journey ended, he had been in many other porno films, been paid as a prostitute, and used cocaine whenever it was available. That he ever made it back home is due to the miraculous work of God and his parents' hard work. We'll look at what they did later in this chapter, after we examine why runaways leave home.

Why They Run

Children run away either because they no longer have homes or, as mentioned earlier, because they believe the problems at home are unresolvable. They don't have the emotional resources to handle what's happening at home. Their situations become so oppressive emotionally that they feel there's no chance there to succeed or survive.

The Bible warns parents against doing anything

that would provoke or exasperate their children. But that's usually what happens in the homes of runaways. The children believe their parents are immovable objects who don't care about them or their feelings. They feel that they are being treated as objects or possessions and, in desperation, they break free. Since they move out impulsively, they rarely "plan out" a runaway attempt. Primarily they run *from* something, not *to* somewhere. Thus, they leave unprepared for the dangers they'll face. Their journeys are almost always extremely underfunded.

Abuse is usually a key factor in their decision to run. This abuse comes in many forms. Most female runaways have been sexually abused. Some have been emotionally beaten down through neglect or by hypercritical parents. Others felt trapped as they watched their parents lose themselves in substance abuse—alcohol and drug addiction. Some are beaten physically, and their runaway journey is literally a run for life.

When runaways leave because of sexual abuse, that abuse usually began at an early age, typically by family authority figures who scared the children into keeping their "little secret" so that no harm would befall their families. As the children reach adolescence and seek to separate themselves from their families, they feel caught in an emotional vise with the perpetrators. The children feel hopelessly trapped, and often the only solutions seem to be suicide or running away. The fact that they run indicates that they want to live. If they are found, their desire to live can be used to bring them home if they can be assured that things will be better.

Runaways Versus Throwaways

There's a difference between runaways and throwaways, although both types of children usually end up in the same situations.

Debbie became a throwaway at age 16. She had a younger sister who was eight years old and a six-month-old half brother. Her mother had remarried, and now her mother's life revolved around the baby and new husband. Debbie's sister was included in the family life now and then, but not Debbie. She always felt like the fifth wheel . . . a burden . . . and was ignored physically and emotionally.

One day, the fears Debbie had been feeling for some time were confirmed by her cruel, selfish mother. "There is no room for you," her mother explained, and then asked her daughter to leave. "You're 16 now. You can get a job to take care of yourself." But Debbie knew there was plenty of room in her mother's house. There was just no room in her mother's heart. So Debbie left.

A certain percentage of runaways are actually throwaways or pushouts like Debbie. These teens are no longer wanted by their parents. Their legal care-takers, often stepparents, have asked them to leave or forced them out of the house. It's not unusual to discover that these parents are young and/or imma-ture and feel little responsibility for themselves or their children.

Where Do Runaways Go?

Runaways who come from split or blended families—those with divorced parents or stepparents, half brothers, half sisters—rarely run away on their own to big cities. More often they will leave home and move in with friends or relatives with whom they feel a sense of belonging. If they don't find new families in this way, runaways may move to the streets. If they're fortunate, people from an emergency shelter or similar group will reach them before they get trapped in street life.

Runaways generally stay within the cities or counties of their homes and return within three days. If the runaway travels far, major metropolitan areas such as Chicago, New York, Miami, Houston, and Los Angeles are the destinations of choice, depending on the season of the year.[5]

A United Way Planning Council study of Los Angeles County suggested there were 10,000 runaways in that county alone on any given day. Experts, in general, believe there may be between 20,000 and 25,000 homeless children in the state of California on any given day.[6]

Dangers on the Street

Life on the street isn't easy for anyone, and it's even more difficult for children under age 18 to stay alive and out of trouble. The basic necessities of life—food, clothing, and shelter—often determine the choices kids on the street will make. More than likely, providing the basic necessities includes prostitution, drugs, pornography, and worse.

John, who left home when he was 18, illustrates where the dangers of the street often lead. He was a good-looking teenager who most people would have thought had it all. His parents planned to help with college tuition. He had the grades and the SAT scores to attend almost any college. He had been accepted at two schools. But his self-destruct mode kicked in, and he set off on a one-man adventure to rid himself of his parents' influence.

From the outside, his mother and father looked like model parents. But things weren't as they seemed. His dad demanded that the family attend every church service. No other event was allowed to take the place of church. There were no exceptions. John's dad didn't have a relationship with God; he had a relationship with church.

The family lived their lives to look good in the eyes of the church. John was often disciplined and frequently heard the words: "What would other people think?" The discipline was always harsh, far beyond what any of his friends experienced. His parents had spanked him appropriately when he was young, but as he became older, what had been disciplining turned into beatings. Wounded by the harsh discipline, John couldn't live up to the standards his parents crammed down his throat. The perfection they sought was beyond his ability to deliver. So, rather than continue to try and fail, he set out on a mission to succeed another way, not realizing that his way would almost guarantee failure.

John hated his mom and dad. In their attempts to make him good, they forgot to help him be human. They hid behind their religion and good works. Justifiably, he felt the church was the most important thing to his parents and that he was just a pawn used to support the picture of the perfect family. *When I leave,* he thought, *I'll be able to blow the image apart.* The desire to hurt his parents and the need to be free of their demands led him to part company in what he thought would be a separation for good and forever.

He took the car his dad had bought him, most of his clothes, and the money he had been saving since he was 10. In the middle of the night, he headed for Los Angeles, a place that looked warm and full of opportunity. He didn't stop driving until his feet were in the sands of the Pacific. There he started life away from parental influence, a life where he could be who he wanted to be.

John's mother and father never found out that their son was gay. Not only was he leaving their stiff discipline, but he was also going to where he thought others would understand the lifestyle he wanted to live. He thought he'd be loved and accepted.

The result? John was accepted into a group of guys who took every cent he had to feed their drug habits. With no money and only his good looks to go on, he became a male prostitute who was popular with all the bisexual men who had families and appeared to be respectable in their communities. He was even being paid to have sex with men who had the same profile as his father. He hated every minute of it, but once he became locked into the system, he couldn't get out. He never did, until he died from AIDS that he contracted from someone's husband. His parents never knew the cause of his death. They only knew that he died years after leaving home.

John's parents are just two of thousands of parents who have had to live with the heartache of lost children. It's a hopeless feeling, a loss that's hard to move beyond. It's a loss so hard to bear that it's worth doing whatever possible to prevent it.

John's story is similar to what happens to many young people who succumb to the dangers on the street. Within three months of leaving home, more than 60 percent of runaways are using drugs regularly, including alcohol, marijuana, cocaine, crack, hash, and heroin. To support their habits, these young addicts eventually have to sell drugs or their bodies.

Pimps prey on runaways, often seeking them out at bus and train stations. Two out of three runaways end up supporting themselves through prostitution—even males. Men who seek out male prostitutes increasingly choose young, inexperienced males just like John to lessen the risk of AIDS.

You Can Make a Difference

We both know a young mother who has to live with the memory of her lost 14-year-old daughter who fled the abuse of her stepfather. Although the mother knew the relationship wasn't good, she never dreamed it was intolerable. When the daughter moved out, her mother searched for her on the streets of Los Angeles. She showed a photograph of her daughter to a thousand strangers, some of whom said she looked familiar. After weeks of searching, she finally found someone who knew her daughter.

The lead directed her to an abandoned building, where she found her daughter living with other runaways in the midst of dirty needles and filth of every kind. The brokenhearted mom pleaded unsuccessfully for the girl to come home. Eventually, the young girl died of a drug overdose. Her grieving mother has a lifetime of regrets to overcome. She is a reminder that we all need to do whatever we can to prevent this trauma. Waiting until our children run away is too late.

When Someone Else's Child Runs Away

If you know parents whose child has run away, you can be of great support to them. They are most likely ashamed, confused, and full of pain. A nonjudgmental friend may be their only source of peace and encouragement. You could become the bridge to God's peace for these people. Just being there, coming alongside them, may mean more than anything you could ever say.

A time may come when you think you can give them some direction. It's important that you encourage them to find the child while also helping them deal with their guilt. Organizations will help them search for their child. Listed in the yellow pages of most large cities, these organizations will want a photograph and other information about the child. Knowing that their parents care enough to search for them is sometimes enough to bring lost children back.

One of the greatest services you can do for the hurting parents is to encourage them to obtain counseling. If their child doesn't come home, they will need professional help in dealing with the guilt and loss. The fact that the parents are obtaining counseling may motivate their child to return home if the child makes contact. A caring counselor may help the parents make it through the trauma and initiate needed changes that will lead to the reuniting of the family.

Encourage the parents to attempt to contact their child. If they take this step, they will need the help of an organization that helps kids on the street. Such an organization can not only help the parents find the child, but can also help the parents say and do appropriate things if contact is made. Most parents who contact their kids feel so guilty that they fall into the trap of providing a quick fix, like sending money. However, a runaway child is making terrible decisions. No amount of money will change the direction he or she is headed. The money will be spent on drugs, most likely, and will only delay resolution of the problem. Discourage the parents from doing anything other than searching for the child through an organization equipped to locate runaways, offering words of love and encouragement if they are able to contact their child, and providing an open invitation to return home.

If Your Child Runs Away

Not all runaways come from terrible homes. Some get involved with the wrong crowd or negative friends and leave just for the thrill or excitement. Although their parents most likely could have taken steps to prevent the situation from occurring, their homes may be as normal as thousands of others in which no one runs away.

Seek Counseling

Having a child run away is a difficult reminder that we all have problems. None of us, no matter how strong our faith, is immune to the problems of this world. If your child leaves, you may vacillate between feelings of relief that he or she is gone . . . and feelings of extreme guilt that you pushed the child to leave . . . and feelings of fear and failure. Whatever your feelings, it's vital that you seek counseling to help you work through them. This is not the kind of problem you can handle alone. With a counselor's help, you may be able to say the right things if contact is made with your child rather than making matters worse on your own. Don't do something you'll regret forever just because you didn't have the courage to get help for yourself.

Although your family may not be riddled with tremendous problems, your runaway child may have created an image of a troubled family. This is important to accept if you want your child to come home. If your child believes that everything will be the same as before, he or she won't be motivated to try again.

At a minimum, you must assure the child that family members will obtain counseling and that there will be hope for new relationships between all family members. If others in the family won't go for counseling, assure the child that you will.

Turn to Others for Help and Support

At this time, it's important for you to have others who'll stand with you. Agencies to help find your child, along with a strong counselor, will help you survive. It may also be helpful for you to seek out a support group of other parents who are living through the same nightmare. These groups can often be found by contacting a local church or social service agency in your community.

Take Action

Just feeling guilty about your child's departure will be destructive for you and may hurt your chances of being reunited with your child. Accepting responsibility and doing what you can to bring the child home, on the other hand, may not only bring him or her home, but may also be the beginning of healing within your family. Let any guilt you feel motivate you to take action. That's what happened in Robert's case. When Robert left, his father first spent a few days justifying his treatment of the boy. But when guilt set in, Robert's dad was determined to find his son.

He went to Los Angeles and contacted an organization called Angels of the Night. He took Robert's picture to as many places as he could. He posted notices that he was looking for Robert. He placed a personal ad in the classifieds. Each notice or ad gave Robert the message that things could be different, that they could work through their problems. Finally, one of Robert's fellow actors met Robert's father in a coffee shop. When Robert's dad showed him the picture, the friend said he'd tell Robert his father was looking for him. Later, the friend also gave Robert the message that things at home really could be different.

So Robert called home. His mother answered, and they cried together. She told Robert that his father was determined to make things work if he'd be willing to come home and start over. Robert and his father met, and Robert agreed to go home. He got into the car and left everything he had behind. He wanted to start all over, to wipe the slate clean. That wasn't totally possible, however, because Robert had added a few very destructive behaviors to his repertoire that were not quickly or easily abandoned. But through family counseling, they did become a family again. Robert's father, who felt as if the reunion was a gift from God, was determined not to destroy the opportunity God had given him. He worked hard to make changes, while Robert worked to heal the scars from the street. Although he was never the same as he had been before, Robert never returned to the street.

This story could be your story. If your child has run away, take heart in the fact that many families are eventually reunited. Pray. But don't just pray. Seek help from those who are dedicated to getting kids off the street.

If you are in need of assistance with a runaway child, the following resources may help.

Runaway Hot Line, Austin, Texas 800/231-6946

Hit Home 800/448-4663

Covenant House 9 Line 800/999-9999

National Runaway Switchboard 800/621-4000

Missing Children HELP Center 800/872-5437

CHAPTER FOURTEEN

Eating Disorders

We work with many good kids. Often these good kids have feelings that aren't so good, and they don't know what to do with them. Some of these good kids feel out of control. They'd never medicate their feelings with drugs. While other kids might rebel, these kids never consider it because rebellion wouldn't look good. So they do the least offensive thing to medicate their pain or exhibit control over an area of their lives no one else can influence. They turn to food as a drug and use their weight to control the family. These good kids feel bad. Their bizarre behavior and distorted shapes are ways of begging for help.

One of these good girls is 13-year-old Rachel. She is five feet six inches tall, weighs 98 pounds . . . and feels like the fattest girl in the eighth grade. She frequently divides the food on her plate in half and in half again, and then eats only half of what's left. Other times, she skips meals entirely. She says she feels disgusting and obese. She hasn't had a period for three months. Everyone tells her to eat more.

Rachel has an eating disorder. She's an anorexic.

Sam is five feet five inches tall and weighs 220 pounds. He used to weigh eight pounds more but went on a diet. His mother is obese, and she never encouraged him to watch what he ate. As the ridicule over his size increased, Sam decided to go on a diet and get the weight off. At a party where they were serving chocolate donuts, Sam wolfed down six donuts before he realized what he was doing. Embarrassed and filled with guilt, he went into the bathroom, stuck his finger down his throat, and forced himself to vomit. Relieved, he went back out to the party, pleased to have discovered a new way to get rid of unwanted calories.

A week later, Sam brought home a pint of his favorite ice cream when his parents weren't around. He downed the whole thing in one sitting and went into his bathroom to force himself to throw up again. A week after that, while his parents were gone, he bought two pints of ice cream and repeated the episode. Three days later in class, Sam made plans to buy a box of chocolate donuts and have a secret celebration—to be followed by his novel calorie-removal system.

Sam has an eating disorder. He's displaying the symptoms of bulimia.

What Is an Eating Disorder?

Eating disorder is a term used by medical or mental-health professionals to describe a person's obsession with food, weight, or inappropriate eating behavior. Since most people change their habits when they become ill or obsess over food during certain times, such as the holidays, this term applies only to those who suffer from obsession and compulsion with food over a long period of time. When speaking about eating disorders, health professionals primarily refer to anorexia, an emotional disorder involving self-starvation that produces a very thin body, or bulimia, a related disorder in which a person develops a pattern of gorging and purging (usually through self-induced vomiting).

In both of these problems, the kids involved use strange ways to lose weight. Some methods are life threatening, such as when kids exercise to the point of exhaustion and chemical imbalance and have to be hospitalized to be restored to physical health. Others binge and then purge the food with high doses of laxatives. The most common forms of quick and unhealthy weight loss are starvation and vomiting.

Incidents of anorexia nervosa and bulimia have more than doubled since 1970. Treatment for eating disorders is complex and can take several years, since it involves physiological treatment as well as psychological and spiritual issues.

Both bulimia and anorexia can be fatal. Common by-products, which we'll look at in more detail later, include damage to reproductive organs, abnormal heart and metabolic rates, and heart and kidney failure. Karen Carpenter is probably the most famous anorexic. She had gone so long without food that her body had started to feed off its own muscle tissue. Since the heart is a muscle, it was damaged by her starvation, and she died when her heart could no longer function normally.

Anorexics are easier to identify than bulimics because they lose more than 25 percent of their body weight. They look like prisoners of war. They are walking skeletons who turn away from food whenever possible. Whereas anorexics shun food, bulimics are obsessed with it.

Because bulimics may maintain a more desirable weight, they aren't easy to identify physically. Some bulimics experience no radical changes in shape or size, but most will become extremely overweight as they lose the ability to manipulate their weight. Both anorexics and bulimics are often sick because refusing food or binging on unhealthy foods and purging the food from the body through exercise, laxatives, or vomiting is destructive to bodily systems.

Denial by parents is a major factor in maintaining children's eating disorders. A parent will often see some warning symptoms but will rationalize them away with thoughts like, *This is just a stage my daughter is going through*. If parents knew how deadly the problem is, they'd never rationalize it away. The fatality rate is 20 percent for victims who suffer from either eating disorder for several years. Patricia Perry, director of the Eating Disorders

Clinic in Toronto, Canada, pointed out that "this [fatality rate] is the highest rate for any psychiatric disturbance." [1]

Who's at Risk?

As mentioned earlier, kids who suffer from eating disorders are usually not the same ones who run on the streets or do drugs. These are the "good" kids, often the ones who go to church and seem to have made the most of their personal lives. Intelligent, accomplished, and usually attractive young women between the ages of 12 and 20 who come from white, upper-middle-class families are most apt to have eating disorders. Usually, these young women (and sometimes men) have a distorted sense of their body image. They consistently talk about looking and feeling fat, even though they may be 15 to 25 percent underweight.

Despite the association these disorders have with the current obsession with being thin, they aren't caused so much by bizarre dieting habits as they are by emotional problems. Frequently, children who have eating disorders are "people pleasers." Their need to please others, even at their own risk, becomes an overriding obsession. They demonstrate patterns of perfectionism and high achievement—perfect grades at school and a desire to be the perfect child at home.

Despite their accomplishments, these children have a poor self-image and low self-esteem. When they reach adolescence, they're tired of having to please their parents and teachers and want to assert their independence while remaining in everyone's good graces. For anorexics, not eating definitely becomes an issue of control. The result is a passive assertion against their parents through control over their own bodies. They choose this because it appears to be the area the parents can control the least.

Most mental health experts believe that young people who suffer from eating disorders haven't matured emotionally and develop bulimic or anorexic behavior as a means of socially or psychologically avoiding responsibility, thereby ensuring their parents will care for them and treat them like children. Patricia Perry further explained that anorexics often have difficulty transitioning from childhood to adolescence, while bulimics often have trouble transitioning from adolescence to adulthood.

The classic anorexic begins her behavior just as her body is maturing sexually and literally stops her physical development in its tracks—including menstruation. The classic bulimic often is emotionally and psychologically immature compared with his or her peers. "I have patients," Perry said, "who say they feel like 10 going on 40. They have handled so much stress while being profoundly immature." [2]

If we believe that life truly makes sense, we must assume that there are reasons eating disorders develop. Things aren't right in the kids' families. Typically, their families include such dysfunctional behavior as overprotection, rigidity, few or no communication skills to resolve conflicts or express emotion, and the use of one or more of the children to diffuse parental conflicts. Unable to identify or express their feelings, children turn to the one thing they can control and manipulate—their weight. Their actions must be considered a cry for help.

More Facts About Eating Disorders

- It's estimated that anorexia and bulimia affect up to 5 percent of the female population of North America and Western Europe.[3]
- In America, six to eight million people suffer from anorexia or bulimia; 90 percent of them are women.
- From 5 percent to as high as 20 percent of all American young women manifest at least one symptom of an eating disorder.
- Twelve percent of college-age females suffer from eating disorders.
- Girls in high school face the highest risk of becoming anorexic.
- Six to 10 percent of anorexics literally starve themselves to death.
- It is estimated that between 2 and 5 percent of anorexics commit suicide.[4]

Let's take a deeper look into anorexia and bulimia.

Anorexia Nervosa

The Diagnostic and Statistical Manual of Mental Disorders (DSM-IV), the handbook used by most mental-health professionals to determine the exact nature and extent of anorexia nervosa, distinguishes the disorder by the characteristics listed below. These are excellent indicators to use in determining if your child has this problem:

- an intense fear of becoming obese that doesn't diminish as weight loss progresses
- a distorted body image, claiming to "feel fat" even when emaciated
- a weight loss of 25 percent of original body weight (or for teens, original weight loss plus projected weight gain based on appropriate growth charts)
- a refusal to maintain body weight
- no known physical illness that would account for weight loss[5]

Only one-third of anorexic teens are even mildly overweight before the onset of this problem. This eating disorder isn't about weight—weight loss or weight control. It's about emotions, control, and self-concept.

Anorexic kids are often perfectionists who set impossibly high standards yet have low self-esteem. They can't handle normal pressures or severe stresses, so they work to control other elements in their lives such as weight and diet. They may also use grades, clothing, and any other area in which they can exert control until their desire for control becomes an obsession.

Joan Jacobs Bramberg, in her book *Fasting Girls*, chronicled the identification of the problem by two doctors in England and France more than 100 years ago. She pointed out that "by returning to its origins, we can see anorexia nervosa for what it is: a dysfunction in the bourgeois family system."[6] She demonstrated that even a century ago, anorexia had its roots in issues of control and independence.

A girl approaching the age of sexual development requires independence, individuation, and a sense of her own identity separate from the family. If she is denied the opportunity to grow socially or psychologically on her own, anorexia can allow her to reduce herself physically to the "stage" of a child, requiring special attention from her parents (especially when she looks emaciated or ill). Or anorexia may allow her to assert control over her life in an area that her parents can't manipulate.

"Refusing to eat," said Bramberg, "was not as confrontational as yelling, having a tantrum, or throwing things; refusing to eat expressed emotional hostility without being flamboyant. And refusing to eat had the advantage of being ambiguous. If a girl repeatedly claimed lack of appetite, she might be ill, and therefore entitled to special treatment and favors."[7]

Anorexics typically have a common ritualistic attitude toward eating. They eat the same small meal day after day, followed by an inappropriately long exercise period. Often an anorexic daughter will prepare elaborate meals for her family, yet eat little or nothing herself. Another familiar behavior pattern of an anorexic, as mentioned previously, is the deliberate ritual of dividing food on her plate into increasingly smaller portions. Anorexics typically engage in compulsive behavior such as hand-washing as well.

Health Risks Associated with Anorexia

Besides the threat of death by starvation, there are other real health risks associated with anorexia:

Heart problems. Anorexia can cause a very low heart rate, abnormally low blood pressure, and abnormal heart rhythms. Anorexics like Karen Carpenter can develop heart failure. Anorexics may also develop lung problems due to dehydration.

Osteoporosis. Anorexic females usually stop menstruating as a result of their low body weight and are at high risk for osteoporosis, which can cause brittle bones that are easily broken.

Other illnesses. Anorexics suffer from kidney and liver problems, anemia, and a low white-blood-cell count that puts them at risk of infection.

Brain changes. Anorexia causes the brain to shrink, which in turn causes problems in concentration and can lead to paranoia, temper tantrums, and hallucinations.

Most of the above problems are reversible once normal eating patterns are resumed. However, permanent damage can occur, particularly in long-term anorexics. Two years after recovery, 25 percent of anorexics have not resumed menstruating, nor can they regain their normal body weight. Between 33 and 50 percent also suffer some psychological impairment. If parents are not aware of anorexic symptoms and how serious anorexia is, most likely their children will suffer alone for many years and could reach the point where irreparable damage has been done.

Bulimia

Bulimia, as mentioned previously, is generally identified by a pattern of binging and purging. Typically, a bulimic can consume thousands of calories—even more than forty thousand calories in one day! The typical binge lasts about one-and-a-half hours, in which 3,400 calories are consumed.

To rid themselves of the calories, bulimics engage in self-induced vomiting, which eventually occurs automatically. Other methods of purging include laxatives, diuretics, and emetics. According to one study, as many as 31 percent of bulimic women use laxatives almost daily.[8] Most bulimics start out in a normal weight range—some slightly over, others under the proposed normal weight. Curiously, at least one of the bulimic child's parents or siblings is usually obese. While the anorexic primarily sees herself as fat, the bulimic may have a more realistic assessment of her body shape and yet be far more obsessed with her attractiveness, especially to the opposite sex.

The Diagnostic and Statistical Manual of Mental Disorders (DSM-IV) distinguishes bulimia by the following characteristics:

1. Secret, episodic binge eating.
2. Three of these five behaviors:
    a. Binging on easily ingested, highly caloric food.
    b. Inconspicuous eating.
    c. Termination of such episodes by abdominal pain, sleep, self-induced vomiting, or social activity.
    d. Repeated attempts to lose weight by severely regulating body weight.
    e. Frequent weight fluctuations of 10 pounds or more due to binges and purges. (However, unlike anorexia, these weight losses are never extreme enough to be life threatening.)
3. Awareness that the eating pattern is abnormal and the fear of not being able to stop.
4. Depressed mood, guilt, and self-deprecating thoughts following binges.[9]

Bulimic episodes, according to this handbook, are not related to anorexia nervosa. The binges are planned. The food consumed is high in caloric content, usually sweet, and has a smooth texture that's easy to consume quickly. Bulimic binges are not a matter of eating too much of a favorite treat and then worrying about the calories. These binges are eaten secretly or as inconspicuously as possible, with the food being "gobbled" or "wolfed" down fast with little chewing.

Wayne Anderson, a professor of psychology at

the University of Missouri, has identified three factors that most often contribute to bulimia:

Cultural standards. Certainly, our society is preoccupied with weight and diet. On the one hand, America is a land of plenty, where becoming overweight is easy. However, people also are obsessed with becoming thin. This worship of being thin is a major factor in creating bulimia.

Cognitive control loss. The body has a natural need for normal food intake in order to nourish and repair itself. The body also has its own control mechanism that works to regulate body weight. Unfortunately, many bulimics place themselves on needless semi-starvation diets that interfere with this control mechanism. Bulimic behavior occurs when these cognitive controls finally break down.

Personality and temperament. In general, bulimics tend to come from families that have addictive behaviors. They often model the behaviors of other excesses such as overworking, overdrinking, and overeating. The family is often out of control, and the bulimic's weight spins out of control as a direct reflection of the family.

Other researchers add this information about bulimia.

Depression. Researchers theorize that some bulimics may have a physiological disposition toward bulimia, since many bulimics (and anorexics) suffer from clinical depression. Some bulimics respond well to antidepressant drugs that promote serotonin synthesis in the brain, the same reaction created by sugar on which bulimics typically binge. From either source, the result is emotionally soothing. However, it's not clear yet whether depression is the cause or the result of such detrimental eating habits.

Anxiety. Another theory states that anxiety leads to bulimia. Medication works well in relieving the anxiety that many people with eating disorders possess. Successful treatment programs have been developed that treat eating disorders as anxiety disorders. Once their phobic fears subside, the patients tend to return to normal eating patterns.

Health Risks Associated with Bulimia

As in anorexia, there are a number of health risks associated with bulimia. Continual vomiting has three dangers:

1. Weakening and deterioration of muscles, including the real possibility of kidney and heart failure.
2. Rips and tears in the small blood vessels of the esophagus.
3. Tooth-enamel erosion and abscesses of the gums.

The use of drugs and laxatives also creates dangers:

1. Using drugs for purging can cause a drop in

potassium levels and may bring on a heart attack.

2. Laxative abuse may result in the body's being unable to function without a laxative.

3. Colectomies (the removal of the colon) are not uncommon among chronic laxative abusers.

You Can Make a Difference
Look Inside the Family

As parents ourselves, we realize that parents already take too many guilt trips. We don't want to add another one to the list. Parents, however, have the power to change the system that produces eating disorders. In one case we're familiar with, the mother was anorexic and obsessed with her weight. She'd eat no fat and exercised until she literally dropped. She stopped menstruating and suffered electrolyte imbalances. These problems didn't go unnoticed by her 12-year-old daughter, who was about 50 pounds overweight and the butt of many cruel jokes at school. She was eating in reaction to what her mother was doing. Out of a desire to develop her own identity and separate herself from her mother, she gained weight. Before the little girl could be helped, her mother needed help for her obsessions.

The good news for parents is that there is hope for our children. The tough news is that hope may begin by our taking on the hard task of working on ourselves first, then helping our children. To be blunt, it's hard for a 360-pound parent to help a 250-pound teenager deal with the problems that have caused the obesity.

Early Detection

As a parent, you probably realize it's normal for teenagers to be worried and even preoccupied with their looks and image from time to time. However, when this phase extends past middle- or late-adolescence, or if your teenager exhibits specific behaviors such as those listed below, suspect anorexia or bulimia and contact a center that can treat the problem and assist you in motivating your child to seek help.

- marked weight loss with no physical explanation
- ritualistic eating patterns
- unreasonable amounts of strenuous exercise— especially right after meals
- medically unnecessary use of laxatives or Ipecac. Ipecac induces vomiting in poison victims; repeated use has a cumulative effect on the heart that can lead to cardiac arrest.

Seek Treatment

Anorexics will deny their illness and usually resist therapy. Hospitalization may be necessary if they have maintained a weight loss of more than 25 percent for more than three months. Bulimics, on the other hand, usually are relieved when their "secret" is out and can be dealt with. However, they often experience depression if their recovery isn't easy and quick. Hospitalization may be necessary if severe binging and purging has upset their metabolism to a dangerous degree or if vomiting has become an involuntary action.

Instill Correct Values

You can help your children avoid eating disorders by encouraging them to pursue positive qualities other than a pleasing physical appearance. Teach them to recognize that being thin, in and of itself, is not necessarily healthier and doesn't demonstrate innate cleverness or superiority. As parents, we do our children an immense disservice if we portray thinness as a symbol of achievement, success, and independence. No one wants his or her child to be fat. But ensuring a child is not 10 pounds overweight is never worth the pain and grief a child, and ultimately the whole family, experiences when he or she wants to be thin at any price.

Hold on to Hope

If your son or daughter suffers from an eating disorder, there's tremendous help available. Hundreds of resources are available to the child who is too thin or too fat. If food has become a source of control or self-medication, there's a way out. Don't consider this to be a phase or a stage. Seek wise counsel, and move your child toward restoration of a healthy self-image. It's always difficult to ask "outsiders" for help, but the results will be worth it.

The central theme of everything we have tried to

say is that though you love your children deeply, love alone may not be enough to raise healthy kids in an unhealthy society. Healthy kids require healthy parents willing to pay a hefty price of self-sacrifice and, perhaps even more painful, self-examination.

The area of eating disorders affects many families. Often one parent has an unhealthy value that says, "You can't be too thin," while the other parent may be overweight. It is very difficult for a child caught in this situation to have a balanced view of weight control.

We encourage you to look at your children. If you find the symptoms we've presented above, purpose to help your child. Before you look at what the child eats as the source of the problem, look at what you think about food and what you believe about weight and thinness. Your attitude may be fine, but if it needs adjusting, be willing to admit it. It is at this foundational level that hope for our eating-disordered children begins. When we adjust our beliefs, the children often adjust theirs. Unless you begin at the beginning, the results of any change in weight may only be temporary.

CHAPTER FIFTEEN

Five Positive Parenting Principles to Prevent Crisis

It had been one of those weeks! Jim and Cathy's kids all decided to go "ballistic" at once. Christy told them they didn't love her anymore. Rebecca refused to go to church. Heidi said she wanted new parents. Jim and Cathy missed their much-needed date night because the baby-sitter canceled 10 minutes after she was supposed to arrive. They were both tired, tense, and needy. That's when they decided to talk with two older and wiser people in their church. This couple had raised three kids successfully and had juggled a busy ministry and home life.

Ben and Carla invited the Burnses to dinner, where Cathy and Jim described their burdens. As they discussed their issues, Ben and Carla laughed. "We had expected wisdom, insight, and understanding, but all we received was laughter," Jim said later.

"The more we said, the more they laughed. Finally, I asked, 'What's so funny?'"

Ben's response was a treasure: "Welcome to life." Ben and Carla offered no quick fixes, no easy answers, and no miracle cures that evening, but they did give Jim and Cathy permission to struggle and have horrible weeks. "When Cathy and I left their home, we felt deeply cared for and, above all, understood. Ben and Carla's advice was simple yet profound."

In this chapter we offer five practical and positive parenting principles. Yet we know that hugs, laughter, and reassurance might be more effective. Parenting isn't easy. Life is difficult at times. But through the years, these five principles have prevented crises in our homes.

1. Take time to relax and enjoy each other.
2. Discipline with consistency.
3. Express affection.
4. Build up a shaky self-image.
5. Love each other.

Let's look more closely at each of those in turn.

Take Time to Relax and Enjoy Each Other

Rest heals, soothes, and gives perspective. Why is it that, in a world of instant everything and more time-saving gadgets than all of us can possibly use, we're usually stressed for time? Let us tell you a story that will help you see we have not yet learned to take time to enjoy one another at one of the most special times of the year—Christmas.

A few years ago, Jim and Cathy's annual Christmas evening discussion went something like this:

Cathy: We've got to do it differently next year.

Jim: I bought all my presents on Christmas Eve AGAIN!

Cathy: We haven't had a free weekend in six weeks.

Jim: I can't believe I'm going to work tomorrow when I'm totally exhausted.

They then promised that next year they would control their schedule and buy presents earlier. "Next year," they said, "we'll spend more time with the kids and less time cooking, cleaning, and decorating. Next year, we'll begin to build special holiday traditions for the girls."

The next Christmas, Jim and Cathy found themselves busier than ever. Christmas Eve was a blur. The only rest they got was during the hour-long Christmas Eve service at church. But even during the celebration of the Lord's birth, Jim was planning their traditional Christmas Eve Chinese-takeout dinner, and Cathy remembered that she forgot to wrap a present for one of the nine people coming to their home after the service. Cathy and Jim breezed through dinner, gifts, cleaning, preparing Christmas stockings, and completing other necessary tasks to prepare for Christmas Day. Then they dropped into bed at 12:15, too exhausted even to talk with each other.

At 4:47 A.M., Christy wandered into their room and asked, "Is it time yet?"

"No!" Jim replied.

At 5:54 A.M., Christy brought Rebecca, whom she had awakened, and climbed into bed to get Jim and Cathy in the Christmas spirit. It didn't work. They told the two girls not to wake Heidi. At precisely 6:01 A.M. (thank goodness for digital clocks), all three girls, including Heidi ("We didn't wake her up, Mommy. She just woke up by herself when we jumped on her bed!"), staged such a major protest that Jim and Cathy had to get up. After they opened stockings and presents and cleaned up the mess (no easy task), they started on breakfast. After breakfast and a quick reading of Luke 2, Jim and Cathy cleaned the dishes and started preparing Christmas dinner.

Cathy and Jim worked fast and furiously, too busy to talk to each other or the girls. When Jim's parents arrived, Jim and Cathy just kept cooking. When other family members arrived, they served "Cathy's finest meal" and ate standing up half the time. Then on to more presents, cleaning up, dessert, cleaning up, putting away the presents, making phone calls, running to the store, and more cleaning up.

It was past time to put the kids to bed and do PJs, teeth, faces, potty, drinks of water, medicine, more drinks of water, prayers, stories, screaming, negotiating, begging, threatening, drinks of water, and preparing to give up. Finally, it was quiet. Just for good measure, Cathy and Jim did some more cleaning. At last they sat down on the couch to watch the end of their favorite Christmas movie, *It's a Wonderful Life*. Cathy fell asleep in 10 minutes. Jim, probably overtired, hungry, depressed, sick, or who-knows-what, cried like a baby through the last half hour of the movie. Stumbling into bed, both Jim and Cathy mumbled, "Next year, it's going to be different. . . . Next year."

You can call it crazy. You can call it insane. But the truth is, most parents today are just too tired to do proactive parenting. One of the major problems with families is the breathless pace at which we live our lives. You can see from the story above that the Burns family is no exception, and neither is the Arterburn family.

Overcommitment and fatigue are two of the greatest distractions from positive parenting. Our children need our time and attention. We both tried to remember special meals (such as Christmas dinner) we had as children. We couldn't remember much about the meals. (Sorry, Mom!) What we really remember and treasure are the times our parents took time to play with us—whether it was Dad throwing a ball in the backyard or Mom having something better to do but playing a game at the kitchen table one more time.

Here's our advice: Parents, quit working so hard. Save energy for yourselves and your family. If it means moving to a smaller house or making a smaller car payment, then do it. Life's too short to settle for fatigue, lack of intimacy, and busyness in the place of meaningful relationships with your spouse and children.

What are you doing this week that will be an absolutely enjoyable experience for you and your children? If you don't have a plan, stop what you're doing and create one. Time is too short not to celebrate with your family. What'll stop you from relaxing a bit and enjoying your kids? The dishes can wait. The yard can wait. Turn off the TV. Grab a few moments of joy and laughter. It may be the best investment for keeping your children away from future disaster.

Discipline with Consistency

Discipline is a training process. The primary purpose of parental discipline is to teach responsibility rather than to evoke obedience. This means consistently helping our children understand that most of life involves choices and consequences. Discipline in the home should consist of setting clearly defined limits with our children. The vast majority of kids we meet in crisis claim not to clearly understand family limits. Most of those kids come from homes where discipline isn't consistent.

To prevent crises in their homes, parents need to emphasize consequences. From the earliest ages through adulthood, we all live with consequences — some good and some bad. When it comes to family issues, the consequences almost always are the results of our actions. If a child runs through the house and breaks a vase, the best discipline is having to clean up the mess and help pay for a new vase. When the act is outright defiance, parents should not be afraid to appropriately use a stronger form of discipline. The consequence for attitudinal rebellion should be quick, clear, and felt. If parents fail and allow rebellion to go uncorrected, when the child becomes a teenager, he or she will have difficulty understanding that rebellion will result in not-too-pleasant consequences.

Tips for Consequences

As kids understand that their actions have consequences, they learn to live life properly.

Consequences should match the problem. To ground Jimmy for a month because he didn't eat all his broccoli is too strong, but to give him a two-minute "time out" when he deliberately slugged his baby sister for the sixth time isn't enough.

Involve kids in consequential decision making. One of the easiest ways to discipline effectively is to include your children in determining consequences. Help them set valid expectations for their behavior. Kids are often harder on themselves than their parents are.

Sometimes you'll have to negotiate, because you and your kids won't see eye to eye. Even that process can be healthy. Adults become naturally apprehensive about losing parental control, while kids—especially teenagers—fret about being deprived of all freedom. Negotiation usually means rules are more likely to be followed.

Discipline calmly. Our rule is simple. Don't give out consequences when you're angry. You'll say the wrong thing, and then you can't be consistent. Phrases like "You'll never . . ." are often not taken seriously.

Jim recalls an incident from his teenager years, when he had just received his driver's license two days earlier. His mother was thrilled that she would no longer have to serve as chauffeur and that Jim would be able to run errands for her. However, Jim made a big mistake. He went on his first drive-by-yourself date that weekend and was two hours late for his curfew. (To this day, Jim still says it was a misunderstanding.)

To say that his father was angry is an understatement. He immediately revoked Jim's car privileges for four months! Jim was in shock. *No car for four months?* he thought. *That's ridiculous!* However, the next day his mother asked him to drive to the market for an errand. He learned quickly that errands were okay. Then when he needed a ride to a baseball game, his father didn't want to go to the game early, so he threw Jim the car keys and made an exception. After two weeks, his parents forgot about the curfew violation, and Jim was free to drive again.

Overall, Jim's parents did an excellent job of parenting, but they missed on that one. Why? Because the consequence was given in anger. When you're angry, calm down before you say or do something you'll regret. Overkill in discipline emerges from impulsive anger. Kids respond to such anger with fear and loss of respect for a parent. As parents, our goal is to use controlled anger even in maddening situations and then to sit down later and discuss our feelings and concerns with our children.

Make Agreements

Every family will thrive better when there are established limits and consequences for behavior. Gary Smalley discussed a survey in his outstanding book *The Keys to Your Child's Heart* that polled linguists, teachers, pastors, evangelists, and medical doctors. Those men and women were asked about the influences that led to their vocational choices and why they became successful in their respective fields. All said that they came from homes with clearly defined limits.[1] There's the old saying, "He or she who aims at nothing gets there every time." As parents, we must take the responsibility to establish clearly defined acceptable and unacceptable behavior for our children.

The agreement. Jim and Cathy have found it easier to actually list as many rules, limits, and expectations they can. That way no one can come back later and say, "But I didn't know I was supposed to do that." The list is posted on the refrigerator. Their girls are four, six, and eight at the time of this writing, so their expectations and consequences are age appropriate.

Burns' Rules
1. Good table manners.
2. Obedience to parents (or the adult in charge).
3. Be courteous to each other.

Rewards
1. Special TV
2. Special outings
3. Treats and dessert
4. Game or book with Mom/Dad
5. Shopping trip; book, toy, clothes
6. Video store
7. Art project

Consequences
1. No TV in morning
2. Go to bed early
3. No friends over
4. Spanking (never in anger)
5. Time out

Express Affection

During a scary storm with booming thunder and lightning, a six-year-old girl shrieked with fright. She leaped out of bed and ran full speed into her parents' bedroom. Her father, trying to calm her, said, "Don't worry, my little angel. God will protect you."

The little girl snuggled closer to her father and said, "I know that, Daddy, but right now I need some-one with skin on!"

That little girl didn't doubt her heavenly Father's ability to protect her. She just wanted the personal touch and affection of her earthly father's loving embrace.

In a recent study at Boston University, researchers stumbled upon a child-rearing study based on interviews with mothers of kindergarten children in the early 1950s. They decided to follow up and see how the children were faring as adults. After locating and questioning 78 percent of the original group, they discovered that the happiest respondents—those who enjoyed their jobs and their families and had a zest for living—all showed one important characteristic: their parents had been warm and affectionate, generous with hugs, kisses, and play time. The most important predictor of future happiness was not a good education or an upscale home, but physical closeness with parents. Factors such as money, major injuries, or even frequent moves had much less bearing on a child's future happiness than genuine affection.

The Power of Affection

Every household is different when it comes to showing affection. Many parents unconsciously withhold hugs, touches, and embraces simply because "it wasn't done that way when I was growing up." Having few positive role models, they honestly don't know what to do. Even in some of the most caring homes, many parents stop touching their children once the children reach grade school. When they quit touching, an important part of showing God's love also stops.

Recently, a father and mother came to Jim's office. Both parents were deeply concerned about signs of sexual promiscuity they had seen in their 17-year-old daughter. The father mentioned that he felt very uncomfortable showing affection to his daughter. He loved her dearly but seldom told her so, and he couldn't remember the last time he had hugged her. At the possibility of sounding trite, Jim said, "If you don't hug your daughter, someone else with another agenda will gladly do it for you." Children and teenagers (adults, too) need meaningful, loving affection. Sometimes the absence of touch can affect a child so much that he or she spends a lifetime reaching out for embraces. More and more research on sexually promiscuous people points back to deep yearnings to be touched and held.

The Boston University study, as well as others, points to the fact that children need love and affection from a father as well as from a mother. Dr. Ross Campbell asserted, "In all my reading and experience, I have never known of one sexually disoriented person who had a warm, loving, and affectionate father."[2] Unfortunately, in a world filled with violence, sexual abuse, and perversion, parents have shied away from giving their children the blessing of tenderness and touch. In one study at UCLA, researchers found that just to maintain emotional and physical health, men and women need eight to 10 meaningful touches each day.

Our Lord certainly understood the importance of meaningful touch. Even with a hectic schedule and constant demands, He took time out to show affection and love to children.

> People were bringing little children to Jesus
> to have him touch them, but the disciples

rebuked them. When Jesus saw this, he was indignant. He said to them, "Let the little children come to me, and do not hinder them, for the kingdom of God belongs to such as these. I tell you the truth, anyone who will not receive the kingdom of God like a little child will never enter it." And he took the children in his arms, put his hands on them and blessed them. (Mark 10:13-16)

Jesus was a master at communicating love and personal acceptance. He demonstrated that when He blessed and held the children, acknowledging their genuine need. He even understood the importance of a grown man's need for touch. To touch a leper was unthinkable in biblical times. The Law even barred a leper from touching anyone. Yet look at what Jesus did:

A man with leprosy came to him and begged him on his knees, "If you are willing, you can make me clean."

Filled with compassion, Jesus reached out his hand and touched the man. "I am willing," he said. "Be clean!" Immediately the leprosy left him and he was cured. (Mark 1:40-42)

Even before Jesus spoke to the leper, He reached out and touched him. How that leper must have felt when Jesus had the courage to show physical affection to him even though he was an outcast!

As parents, we are often the arms, legs, and mouthpieces of Jesus to our children. During a Burns family prayer time, six-year-old Rebecca began her prayer by saying, "Dear Daddy. . . ." She then looked up, smiled at Cathy and Jim, and said, "I mean, 'Dear God.'"

After the time of prayer, Cathy leaned over to Jim and said, "The 'Dear Daddy, I mean, Dear God' phrase sure has hidden theological meaning, doesn't it?" Rebecca Joy Burns's concept of God is close to her concept of her earthly father. (Let's hope she doesn't think that God is bald and has a mustache like her father!) With God's help, Jim's interest, compassion, discipline, and even his affection will continue to give her a positive, healthy concept of God. As parents and significant adults in the lives of children, all of us should constantly model His love.

Cathy and Jim have come up with a "Daily To-Do List" for their children. This isn't a legalistic list; rather, it's a set of guidelines to help keep their three girls' spirits open and filled with a sense of security and love.

1. *"I love you."* Every day, our children must be reminded of our love. This positive reinforcement and reminder of unconditional love will give them the ability to go on during tough times and say no to temptation.

2. *Physical affection.* It's incredible what a meaningful and appropriate touch, hug, embrace, kiss, or even a "high five" will do to a young person's self-image. Touching brings a real sense of meaningfulness and security.

3. *Listen*. Listening is the language of love. When your kids know you are really listening, they will sense how significant they are to you.

4. *Pray daily.* A daily time of prayer with each child helps him or her know how important God is in your life. The warm memory of holding our girls in prayer will last a lifetime.

5. *Eye contact.* Life gets so busy that we parents often forget that body language and eye contact are special ways of letting children know we care.

Leesa always sat as far away as possible from Jim in his Sunday school class. With her arms folded and a scowl on her face, this 10th-grader was definitely saying that her parents *made* her come to church. Jim doubted if church was on her top-10-things-to-do-on-a-weekend list! She was there every week, but she seldom talked and often combed her bangs over her eyes.

One day after class, Jim decided to go up to Leesa, give her a hug, and tell her he was glad she was in the class. He walked straight up to her, reached out his arms, and hugged her. She never moved, never looked up, and didn't respond. In fact, Jim says it felt like hugging a cold, immovable, metal, pole. He fumbled through his pre-planned speech and walked away feeling like a fool. The next week he tried again. It didn't work any better.

Two years went by, and Leesa seemed to be a little more open but still hesitant. Finally, at a camp sharing time, Leesa stood up to speak. The youth group became especially quiet. No one was used to her giving much more than a two-sentence response to anything. As she stood, tears came into her eyes. "Two years ago, Jim came up to me and gave me a hug," she said. "To my knowledge, no one had ever hugged me since I was a baby. To be honest, most of the time I'm not very huggable. The day he hugged me, I melted on the inside. It has taken me two years to understand what God's love is all about, but tonight I made a commitment to Christ, and I want to thank Jim for hugging me two years ago." That night, Leesa received more hugs than she had received in her entire life.

The lesson was once again quite clear. Sometimes God uses people with "skin" to show children and others how much they are loved by our earthly families and our heavenly Father.

Build Up a Shaky Self-Image

The primary task of the teenage years, some say, is to develop a source of personal self-esteem. Building a positive, healthy, Christ-centered self-image in their children is one of the primary tasks of all parents. Frankly, we have seldom, if ever, seen a kid involved in drug abuse, suicide, or other crisis who has a healthy self-image. The two graphs that follow diagram this better than we can explain it.

The Negative Self-Image Cycle

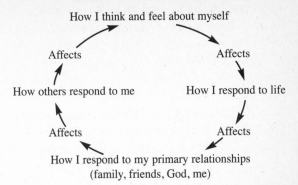

How I think and feel about myself

Affects   Affects

How others respond to me   How I respond to life

Affects   Affects

How I respond to my primary relationships
(family, friends, God, me)

The Inferiority Cycle

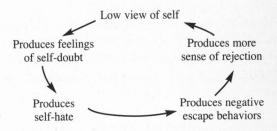

Low view of self

Produces feelings   Produces more
of self-doubt   sense of rejection

Produces   Produces negative
self-hate   escape behaviors

These vicious cycles get worse unless the negative self-image cycle is broken. Today's young people are often torn apart by a brutal world that breaks down self-esteem. Kids as well as adults place a great deal of importance on brains, bucks, and beauty. If we aren't careful, we play the comparison game and come up short every time. There's always someone smarter, richer, and better looking. We can help our children by building up their self-image rather than tearing it down. Children who grow up in an environment full of put-downs, negative nicknames, and criticism often become critical adults whose self-esteem is less than adequate.

The Value of Time

It may sound trite, but the only quality time is quantity time. You can't produce healthy kids by spending only five minutes a day with them. You must make time—special time—to be with your kids.

After trying to have kids for 10 years, Steve and Sandy were blessed with their beautiful baby, Madeline. Steve is determined to do the best job possible in raising her. He's cut back his travel, and when he's in town, he doesn't leave for work before she wakes up. He does no work at home until she's in bed in the evening. Each Thursday night, he takes her out to eat. Steve is attempting to get into the habit of spending lots of time with his daughter. He correctly believes that by giving her quality time, he is making a valuable investment in his little girl's future.

Encourage Your Kids

There's real power in affirmation and encouragement. When will we parents learn that we can motivate children much more effectively through encouragement than through guilt? We've heard it said that it takes nine affirming comments to overcome every negative comment. Our children need us to believe in them, praise them, and be available to them. We've got to catch them doing something right and tell them in order to build up their self-esteem.

Help Your Kids Gain an "Attitude Focus"

Young people are idealistic and extremely hard on themselves. Many aspects of life that kids want to change simply never will. Help your kids learn that although many circumstances won't change, their attitudes can, and that makes all the difference. We love the prayer of Saint Francis of Assisi: "God, grant me the serenity to accept what I cannot change, the courage to change what I can, and the wisdom to know the difference."

Check the Physical Warning Signs

We're convinced that poor eating and sleeping habits are at the core of many young people's self-image problems. (For example, more than 50 percent of American high school students are over-weight.) Home should be a place where kids can receive input on proper nutrition, rest, exercise, and other aspects of healthy living. God made the body, mind, and spirit to work together. Ineffective use or function of body, mind, or spirit can significantly reduce a person's positive self-image.

Another suggestion would be to arrange regular physical checkups for your children. Kids often act a certain way because of a physiological problem.

Give Your Kids Success Experiences

Many young people with a poor self-image need a few successes to build their confidence. Sometimes it's something as easy as setting up a tennis tournament so that Bill can show off his ability or asking Janet to use her artistic talent to make a poster. Find ways to help kids experience success. You may need to become a math tutor or spend extra time on the soccer field with your child.

Help Your Kids Practice Thankfulness

Happy people are thankful people. We are challenged by what Paul wrote in Thessalonians: "Give thanks in all circumstances, for this is God's will for you in Christ Jesus" (1 Thess. 5:18).

Recently, a 12th-grade girl with an extremely negative attitude came to talk with Jim. For the first half hour of the conversation, she grumbled and complained her way through every topic she brought up. Although Jim wouldn't suggest that this is always a good counseling technique, he finally stopped her and asked if there was anything in life for which she was thankful. After a long pause, she said, "My car." He then told her he was going to introduce her to what he called "thank therapy." He asked her to take a piece of paper and a pencil and write at least 20 reasons she could be thankful. She may not have received a miraculous cure from her bad attitude that day, but she practiced "thank therapy" and walked out of his office a much happier person. Sometimes kids need help in focusing on the reasons they can be thankful rather than on their problems.

Let Your Kids Know That Counseling Can Be a Positive Option

Jim and Cathy recently spoke to a large group of single adults on the subject of proper self-image. Cathy told the group that involvement in a counseling relationship had been extremely helpful for her self-image. She and Jim had been infertile for eight years. After numerous operations and years of frustrating doctors' visits, Cathy sought counseling to help her through the hurt and pain of infertility.

After she told her story, Jim and Cathy were amazed at the number of people who asked questions about counseling. They were also surprised by the number of people who said, "I'm so happy to hear that a pastor's wife needed counseling, too!" When you look at the stress-filled situations in which young people find themselves today, consider counseling an important option for help.

Get Your Kids Focused Outside Themselves

Kids with a low self-image are extremely self-absorbed. There's so much going on inside their own lives that they have little desire to reach outside themselves. Yet when kids are challenged to serve and become other-centered, their self-image will improve. Use every opportunity to get your children involved in missions and service projects. One of the greatest benefits of this kind of involvement is that the kids begin to feel as if they're doing something positive with their lives. Everyone needs to be needed and has a deep desire to be used by God in a special way.

Love Each Other

This principle seems obvious, but at the same time, we realize that half the people reading this book are single parents or have been remarried. And in any case, this is still a key parenting principle. Children are much more secure in their own lives when they know their parents love each other. A relationship in which there is an investment of love, time, and energy is one of the major factors in keeping a family strong. If your marriage is suffering, please seek counseling. We challenge you to stop investing so much of your energy elsewhere and to put it back into your marriage. With the proper amount of work, most marriages can succeed.

John and Linda's marriage, for example, was rapidly falling apart. They were putting no energy into the relationship. The little energy left over from their extremely busy lifestyle was devoted to the kids, but their kids' lives were also falling apart. So John and Linda came to us for counsel about their kids. We basically told them, "There's very little we can do to help your kids unless you work on your marriage." They affirmed their love for each other and said that for the sake of the kids, they would focus more on their marriage.

We helped formulate a plan for them, and we offer it to you as well:

- Counseling was a necessity. John and Linda needed a mediator for a while to help them focus on the issues.
- A date night had to become a nonnegotiable part of their week.
- Regular times away were also required. They were to choose a weekend getaway every three months. These "second honeymoons" became special times for building their relationship.
- A weekly family worship time was begun. We've observed that family members who pray and worship together tend to have fewer conflicts.
- Fun times were planned. John and Linda turned off the television and started playing games at home. Eventually, the kids joined them for marathon Monopoly nights.

About two years later, we saw John and Linda and mentioned to them that we never did have the opportunity to work on the problems they were having with their kids. Holding hands and smiling, they said, "Ever since we've been doing better, they've been doing better."

As we mentioned at the beginning of this chapter, there are no easy answers or quick fixes. In fact, there are no 100 percent guarantees to a crisis-free family. However, if you work daily on these five simple principles, the chance that you'll need the other material in this book will be greatly reduced.

CHAPTER SIXTEEN

Influencing Young People's Spiritual Values

Michael wasn't a bad kid. In fact, with only a few rough edges, he was basically a really good kid who had lots of potential, good grades, many friends, and a pleasing personality. Jim had known his parents for several months. They were the all-American family: active in church, enjoyed great family times, and had no major turmoil. Michael's sister was "Miss Outgoing and Popular." She was loved and admired at school, church, home, and everywhere! So what could be wrong?

When Michael was 16, he informed his family that he was no longer willing to attend church. He wasn't throwing out all the morals; he simply didn't believe in God and thought church was boring. Six months passed, and he never attended church. His mom and dad were crushed. "Should we force him to go to church with us?" they asked. "What can we do to build his faith? What about family devotions? How can we talk with our kids about God without sounding preachy?" Then his dad asked, "How can I answer his questions about the faith when I keep some of the same questions buried deep inside my own soul?" Those were all good and valuable questions.

Jim met with Michael. He wasn't antagonistic, just unmotivated. Jim looked for deep-rooted issues: major sin, a broken relationship with his parents, abuse, or anything else that might have caused his lack of faith. After a while, Jim said to him, "I think your questioning is healthy."

"You do?" Michael asked.

"Yes, I really do. You are asking great questions for someone your age. Often these questions about the faith don't come up until a person is out of the home, in college, or even later in life."

Michael smiled and said, "You don't think anything is wrong with me?"

"No, I don't," replied Jim. "I think the only thing that would be wrong is if you quit searching for the right spiritual answers. I wonder how much of the fact that you perceive church as boring is related to your attitude and not to the church?" Jim let that question sink in, and then continued, "Are you willing to invest five minutes a day in your spiritual life and meet with me twice a month for three months to talk about any questions you have about your faith or anything else you want to bring up?"

"I'd be really open to that," Michael said.

Jim handed him a devotional book that would take less than five minutes a day to complete in three months, and they set up another meeting. Jim called him twice during the time before they met. Michael was taking Jim's challenge. When they got back together, he had been to church on Sunday, had held several conversations with his parents about their faith, and had prepared a full page of questions— some of which Jim couldn't answer. They talked, laughed, prayed, and set up another meeting.

After only three months, Michael had rekindled his faith. He still had questions and didn't always love the adult-oriented church service. (We don't always love the service, either.) However, he was now committed to Christ and to church. After three months, Jim and Michael stopped meeting because Michael was now getting together with his dad for the same purpose. There's nothing else to say but, "Yahoo!"

Just because young people are bored with the Christian faith doesn't mean they hate God. They may be going through a normal adolescent questioning phase and need a personal relationship with a spiritual mentor. We suggest that parents develop a regular devotional time with their children. This isn't a time for fathers and mothers to preach to their kids, but a time of Bible study and prayer together, within an atmosphere of openness where no questions are considered to be silly.[1]

As we look at the traits of healthy family life, we can't help but mention the spiritual dimension. To be a Christian doesn't mean family problems all go away. It simply means we have God's help and guidance in dealing with issues.

Influencing Spiritual Values

Dr. James Dobson has said, "I believe the most valuable contribution a parent can make to his child is to instill in him a genuine faith in God. What greater ego satisfaction could there be than knowing that the creator of the universe is acquainted with me personally?"[2]

Most of us would agree that there's absolutely nothing more important than imbuing spiritual values and Christian commitment in our children. But this is one of the most difficult tasks of parenting. One woman said, "Homework, curfews, rules, and music class I can handle. The tension for me is the spiritual stuff. I feel as if I'm trying new gimmicks and techniques. It's dull, it's dry, and I feel as if I'm losing the battle. We go for long stretches with nothing, and then I try a new method . . . for a while."

To be perfectly honest, we can't provide magical techniques that will transform kids' spiritual lives. We don't have the perfect product for $29.95. We can't sponsor a special retreat that's guaranteed to transform kids' spiritual lives. We can, however, offer hope, encouragement, and some spiritual principles that have worked through the years.

Parents Set the Pace

Excitement is caught, not taught. Cathy recently asked how Jim became so interested in sports and why he loves the beach. He'd never thought about it logically before, but the answer came easily. "My dad's first love is sports, and my mom would rather be at the beach than just about anywhere else. Many of my most special memories of growing up focus on catching my dad's excitement at an athletic event or enjoying the sunshine, breeze, and waves of the sunny Southern California beaches with my mom." Influential people around us most often shape our attitudes and actions. Many parents and churches have smothered excitement for God by treating Him like a great killjoy or a boring, distant relative.

Recently, we had the privilege of spending time with a roomful of deeply committed Christian teenagers. Though far from perfect, they possessed a radical commitment to Christ, and their faith was ablaze with energy. We asked them point-blank, "What brought you to this point in your faith?" One boy mentioned prayer, several mentioned friends or youth workers, but the vast majority told of their parents' influence. Parents set the pace.

From childhood, we learn best from role models. Principles and methods mean little to a child, but example means everything. What do Mom and/or Dad teach when they drop off their children at church, go to brunch or sit and read the paper, and then pick up the children after church? How about the parent who knows all the right doctrine, never misses a church meeting, but is a tyrant at home? Martin Luther once said, "I have difficulty praying the Lord's

Prayer because whenever I say 'Our Father,' I think of my father, who was hard, unyielding, and relentless. I cannot help but think of God that way."

As children, our earliest concepts of God don't come from a book or church but from our parents. "The Bible is the most important book in the world," we say, but if our children never see or hear us read it, how can they relate to what we say and do?

If our children watch us "cut corners" and compromise integrity in little ways, why won't they think we'd do the same in things that matter most, like our spiritual life? Proverbs 10:9 tells us, "The man of integrity walks securely, but he who takes crooked paths will be found out." This verse implies another step. The man or woman of integrity walks securely, and so will his or her children.

Jim's eight-year-old, Christy, was sitting in a chair in their living room reading her little devotional. When he asked her what she was doing, she said, "I'm pretending I'm Mommy!" Why? Because she sees her mother sit in that same place reading a devotional.

A friend who is a chaplain in our local juvenile hall told us, "A juvenile delinquent is usually nothing but a child who's trying to act like his parents." That's not always the case, but it's probably true most of the time. As parents, we can't relegate our children's Christian education to even the finest church or most excellent youth group. The responsibility lies on our shoulders. It's a privilege and responsibility from God that we must take seriously.

You Can Make a Difference
Talk to Your Kids about God

We have a mutual friend who is an excellent pastor. He does a great job caring for his congregation, and his sermons are usually right on the mark. We have only one minor complaint. It's the way his voice changes whenever he talks about "GAAWD." His casual conversation changes to an extremely formal tone when he emphasizes a spiritual word. Actually, it's funny. Even his wife makes fun of him sometimes.

Often, we meet parents who have the same problem. They communicate well with their kids, but when the conversation turns to spiritual issues, their mouths freeze, their countenances change, and words come out in a manner that the kids only hear when their parents talk about God.

When you talk to your kids about God, be yourself. One friend told us that his best spiritual conversations with his son take place when they're playing basketball. For some reason, when they are at the park "shooting hoops," questions and information flow. It's not forced. Positive results come because of these "spiritual basketball games."

Talking to your kids about God will happen most naturally when your children see your own growing relationship with God. Share with your children what you're learning. Share your victories and disappointments. A spiritual bond and intimacy with your children come when you develop an open, forgiving, and listening atmosphere. Far too many kids believe God is that great killjoy in the sky because their models for the faith—their parents—only mention God in a negative, guilt-producing manner.

Make Life an Adventure

Make it fun to be a follower of Jesus. Jim Rayburn, the founder of Young Life, was fond of saying, "It's a sin to bore a kid with the gospel." That's why we like the idea of building beautiful memories with a spiritual theme.

We know a family that took a week's vacation in the picturesque Yosemite Valley. Daily they hiked to the waterfalls, swam in the rivers, looked for deer, and ate fun food. Every night they played a game they called "I Spy." Every day in Yosemite, all family members had to record 20 ways they saw God working that day in their world. They'd come up with the description of a miraculous waterfall or perhaps the conversation one of the kids had with a new friend who was camping nearby. A fun vacation week turned into a meaningful spiritual time as well.

Regular family times don't have to be dull, either. Too many parents raised in Christian homes remember enduring (with an emphasis on *enduring*) family devotions. They were boring, adult-oriented, and centered on "preaching." Although we aren't Bible scholars, we searched the Bible and decided that it never says family devotions are to be boring! Set aside a special time each week for a family devotional. The Burns household likes to act out Bible stories. They recently attempted the story of the

Good Samaritan. They had to share the roles because, with only five of them, they needed to play different parts. They wanted Jim to be the traveler because they wanted to beat him up. Cathy was the donkey! They simply read the story, acted out each part, and talked about how they could apply this great parable to their lives. Then they prayed. After a devotional like that, Jim's kids won't let him get away with three points and a poem. Right now, his kids actually like their family devotional time.

Build Traditions

Keeping Advent calendars, making regular trips to the convalescent hospital, or simply going around the table every Thanksgiving and giving five reasons why we are thankful can be meaningful. Christian education takes place best during those times. Nonformal, nontraditional settings are usually much more effective in reaching kids. Educators call this "hidden curriculum," learning that takes place outside the classroom. We know a family, for instance, that has memorized the entire book of Philippians while driving on trips. Each time they memorized a chapter, they planned a special family celebration. When they finally memorized the entire book, they bought themselves a new CD player. That's effective spiritual learning.

Become Involved in Family Ministry

We have never seen an academic study on the fact that the family that ministers together stays together.

However, our hunch is that when families are involved in reaching out beyond their own worlds to serve others, they have a stronger spiritual bond. The call to Christ is a call to serve. There's something special about having a heart that breaks from the same things that break God's heart. Something special happens when you allow God to work in and through your life. Every family we know that serves together regularly has a strong foundation and closeness that other families are missing. Here are some examples:

The Rice family lives in San Diego. They save their money all year, and then, at Christmastime, they visit orphanages across the border in Mexico, open the back of their pickup truck, and pass out shoes to barefoot children. On a monthly basis, they return to play games with the children, build, paint, and serve any way they can. They are a close-knit family, and all the kids have a desire to serve God.

The Rigery family weekly dishes up food at a local soup kitchen.

The Johnsons visit a convalescent home once a month.

The Culps have opened their home to drug babies, and the entire family gets involved.

The Swantons have a volunteer workday at the church once a month.

The Burkes have chosen to "adopt" several of the more elderly saints in their church who don't have family members in the area. They take meals, mow lawns, and visit at least weekly. Each child has a special chore.

A teenager, Trevor Ferrell, is literally one of our heroes. He and his family live in a nice suburb of Philadelphia. One night, during the evening news several years ago, the family viewed the horrible plight of homeless people along the streets of Philadelphia. Eleven-year-old Trevor asked his dad, Frank, to take him downtown so he could see firsthand how street people live. He took one blanket and a pillow to give to a needy person. Trevor was so profoundly affected by what he saw that he asked his family to go back regularly. Trevor and his family collected used coats, hats, and other clothes to pass out to his new friends. He convinced local residents to give him soap, coffee, and sometimes sandwiches. Today, Frank and Trevor have started a ministry called Trevor's Army, through which volunteers around the city pass out blankets, food, and—most of all—hope to homeless people.

Family members who minister together create a lifestyle of servanthood. They ask the question, "What can we do for someone else?"

Create a Desire for God's Word

One of our jobs as parents is to plant the Word of God in our children's lives. Here's a great promise:

> All men are like grass, and all their glory is like the flowers of the field; the grass withers and the flowers fall, but the word of the Lord stands forever. (1 Pet. 1:24-25)

How can you create a desire for God's Word in your children?

First, surround your kids with good resources. Children love Bible stories filled with action, such as David and Goliath, the birth of Christ, and Abraham and Lot. There are outstanding Christian resources available today. Even the new Christian video series are top quality. When your children are young, read to them and talk about the scriptural content.

Second, share what you learn from God's Word. Again, don't preach, but through a spontaneous conversation share something you learned from the Bible. This will often motivate your children to learn from the Word.

Third, consistently show your appreciation for the Word. Remember what Paul wrote to the Thessalonians:

> And we also thank God continually because, when you received the word of God, which you heard from us, you accepted it not as the word of men, but as it actually is, the word of God, which is at work in you who believe. (1 Thess. 2:13)

Help Your Kids Recognize That the Bible Isn't Just Any Book; It's the Word of God

At this point, you may be thinking, *These points are all fine, but you don't know my kid. He hates church and will have nothing to do with anything that even comes close to smelling spiritual.* We know it's not easy. Life is complicated, and the issues surrounding our spiritual lives aren't always cut and dried. We want to assure you, however, that it's never too late. Proverbs 22:6 states, "Train a child in the way he should go, and when he is old he will not turn from it." Although that's not a promise or a guarantee, it is a principle that should hold great hope for us.

No matter what happens, don't give up and don't stop praying. You do your part and ask God to do His. In the meantime, the apostle Peter gave us excellent advice that relates well to parenting a child who is not walking with God:

> Humble yourselves, therefore, under God's mighty hand, that he may lift you up in due time. Cast all your anxiety on him because he cares for you. (1 Pet. 5:6-7)

CHAPTER SEVENTEEN

Hope for Parents Who Think They've Failed

About two summers ago, Steve addressed a gathering of musicians and speakers in Pennsylvania. There were thousands of people camped out on the grounds who had come to have their spiritual lives strengthened. After Steve had spoken, a long line of people wanted to talk with him. As is his style, he had only a few minutes or he would be late for his plane. But one by one, he talked with people. As the line dwindled down and the pressure to leave grew greater and greater, he was confronted by a deeply troubled young girl who needed someone to listen to her. Even though he knew he might miss his flight home, Steve listened as the girl unfolded her story. She had done just about everything wrong and made just about every poor decision possible. She had been a prostitute, she had become pregnant, she had been a drug addict, and just before this festival, she had been released from prison. Her parents had not physically or sexually abused her, but they had made some mistakes. She took their mistakes and copied the worst of them. As Steve listened to her story of repeated disasters, one thought crept into his mind: *Her parents have failed.*

It happens. As much as we hate to admit it, one of the harsh realities of life is that parents blow it. Sometimes they fail in their careers, sometimes they fail in their marriages, and sometimes they fail in raising their children. Trying to deny that reality or sugarcoat it does not make it go away. If you are a parent who feels you've failed, you are probably more interested in knowing what to do about the problem than in having someone try to ease the pain by telling you the pain shouldn't be there.

Sometimes it seems that the older we get, the deeper the pain becomes. We wonder how much pain we can endure. We wonder if there is some way to stop the pain.

If you have spent most of your adult life living in pain and feeling like a failure, you can feel differently. It's not too late to change the way you feel. It's not too late to make a difference in your children's lives.

It's Never Too Late to Start

I'm sure you've heard stories of people who learn to do new things late in life. For example, there was an 86-year-old female marathoner in Los Angeles this past year. She was a great reminder that there is a lot of life to be lived, no matter how old we get. What matters is what we decide to do with the time we have left. You may not want to run a marathon, but you can run your life differently.

If you are to live without the pain of failure, you are going to have to do some things differently. Sometimes we get stuck in the same routine. The routine soon becomes a rut. Sometimes our kids see us in our self-designed rut and rebel against it and us because they sense we are stubborn about changing. They carry into their adult lives the idea that we thought we were right about everything.

It's important to let our kids know we are aware of our inadequacies. Tell them. You have nothing to lose in honestly admitting to them that you didn't do everything correctly as a parent. That admission may be the key to opening communication and beginning the process of healing your relationships with your kids. It may be hard for you to admit you made mistakes, but it is an essential part of the healing process.

There is another way to let your kids know you don't think you are perfect. It is also the best way to ensure you don't repeat the mistakes of the past, especially mistakes of communication with your kids. The suggestion we are about to offer is one that has been a constant theme throughout this book. Find a counselor. A counselor can help you resolve your feelings of guilt while also helping you find new behaviors that will ease rather than create hostility.

Maybe you think your kids are too old to be

helped, or that you are too old to change. Those thoughts are self-defeating. Start thinking, instead, of what it would be like to be able to communicate with your kids as healthy adults.

In many churches, people are told that counseling is unnecessary or even unbiblical. Some would say that God is powerful enough to help us without counseling. Proving that observation untrue are many wonderful Christian counselors who have not only studied the Bible, but have also learned how to help you apply biblical truths in your life. Those counselors can provide valuable insight into yourself and your deteriorated relationships. We often need a third party, an objective bystander, to help us see things we don't see ourselves. We have also found that, in many instances, God's power is unleashed through a trained professional counselor.

Finding a counselor is not antibiblical or anti-God. In fact, it is following through on a scriptural principle. Proverbs 15:22 reminds us that we often fail for lack of counsel. If you believe good counsel could have helped you when you first began to raise your kids, accept the fact that getting good counsel now may help you relate to them as they approach adulthood. It's not easy to admit we need help. It's a very humbling experience. But by humbling ourselves, we open the door of God's power to help us.

Hope for the End of Suffering

If you are a parent who feels you've failed, you have already suffered greatly. You have already experienced years of frustration and defeat. Sometimes we become more discouraged than we need to be out of a belief that our suffering will never end. If we believe we will have a life of unending pain, we often lay tracks into the future that almost guarantee our suffering will continue. Be encouraged that this suffering will not last forever.

Once again, the Bible provides us with great assurance. If we look to the Lord as our source of strength and hope, we will find relief for our suffering. Romans 8:18 reads, "I consider that our present sufferings are not worth comparing with the glory that will be revealed in us." That is a clear message of hope to all of us that better days are coming. God is concerned about your suffering. He does not want you to spend your life in pain. There will come a time when your present suffering will mean very little when compared with the great things God will do in your life.

There is also tremendous hope for your children. They, too, may decide to lean upon the Lord. Their suffering, the result of their rebellion and isolation, may also one day be replaced by God's glory.

If you have been suffering silently, take hope that it will not endure. Be patient. One day your pain may be replaced by the sounds of children who have matured and now want to make peace with Mom and Dad. Do what you can to help the relationship, and never lose hope in the God who wants the relationship healed.

Conclusion

Remember the girl at the Pennsylvania festival — the one who caused Steve to stop and think so deeply about parental failure? She still writes to him. Her life is about 300 percent better today than it was then. She is settling into adulthood as a mature person. The spiritual awakening that many others experienced in that open field also came to her life. She rededicated her life to Christ, she ended her years of rebellion, and she started a new life as a responsible human being. Today, as we finish this book, she is making plans to marry a young man who has committed to loving her today and forgetting who she was yesterday.

Her story is a reminder that even though we may fail as parents, there is a God who loves our children more than we do, and He never fails. No matter how many mistakes we parents make, there is still hope that a wayward child will respond to the power of the Holy Spirit, make a decision for Christ, and come back to a life pleasing to God. To that end, we encourage you to never lose hope, never give up, never stop praying.

Even though you may not have been the best parent, even though you do not feel you were successful because you were just trying to survive, and even though you feel you can have no further influence on your children, you can still affect their lives through prayer. Your prayers could well be the key to unlocking years of rebellion and resentment. Have hope! Never give up!

30 Ways to Keep Communication Open with Your Child

1. Ask your child what his or her favorite song is, listen to it, go over the words, discuss what they mean, and ask what makes the song a favorite.

2. Break through superficial conversation by asking some probing questions: "What's going well in your life? What's not going well? What changes would you like to make? What is the biggest challenge you're currently facing?"

3. Ask your child to pick a new sport, hobby, art project, or interest for the two of you to develop together.

4. Take your child out to breakfast with no agenda—and just listen.

5. Visit a rest home together, and discuss feelings about death, dying, and aging.

6. Keep a journal of family highlights and special accomplishments throughout the year. Review it together on December 31.

7. Help your child develop a set of lifetime goals, such as acquiring specific skills, graduating from college, saving $10,000, or marrying a Christian.

8. Tell your child one of your fears, and do something together that challenges your fear. If you fear flying, fly. If you fear water, swim.

9. Share some of the struggles you had when you were your child's age (that may require some digging in your memory!). Then ask your child what his or her struggles are.

10. Ask your child to pick three places he or she wants to visit within driving distance, and make a plan to see them during the next year.

11. When your child returns home after a concert or other event, ask lots of questions (without coming across as nosy or invasive): "What is it that you particularly like about the musician? Is there a theme or message that comes through in the music? Did the musician have anything interesting to say between songs?"

12. Select a classic from literature, and have a family reading time at least once a week.

13. Take your child to work or the place you volunteer for a day.

14. Adopt a grandparent in a nursing home.

15. Ask your child about his or her heroes. Write a letter to the person, and see if you get a response.

16. Ask your child to join you in a study of a foreign country, the eventual goal being to visit that country within five years.

17. Tell your child your family history while you record it on cassette tape or videotape.

18. Celebrate days other than birthdays, such as 10,000 days on earth, 100th month, and so on.

19. Share New Year's resolutions and review them on June 30.

20. Research the meaning of your child's name, and point out the character traits that parallel the name.

21. Write your child a letter, saying what in your life you enjoy, what you don't, how you have succeeded, where you made mistakes, and what you hope he or she can learn from your life.

22. Sponsor a needy child who lives in a foreign country through Compassion International or World Vision.

23. Help your child develop a mission statement for life that reflects his or her values and what he or she hopes to accomplish.

24. Rent a video on human sexuality, and talk about it after you view it together.

25. Visit a jail with a Christian ministry group, and discuss how you could help meet the needs of some of those who are there.

26. Have your child count the number of commercials he or she sees in a week and put them in categories of what's being promoted, such as drinking, sexual permissiveness, or materialism.

27. Develop a relationship between your family and a missionary family your church supports. Pray for them and write to them together.

28. Serve at a soup kitchen together.

29. Record your family tree going back as far as possible. Try to list one or two prominent character traits associated with each family member. See if you can identify patterns that run through your family.

30. Play board games or cards with your child. Use this time to find out what's going on in his or her life.

Endnotes

CHAPTER ONE

1. Carla Koehl, *Newsweek* Special Edition: "The 21st-Century Family," Winter/Spring 1990, 60.

2. Stephen Arterburn and Jim Burns, *Drug-Proof Your Kids* (Ventura, CA: Regal Books, 1995), 29.

3. Jeanne Wright, *Los Angeles Times*, "Stressing the Importance of Abstinence," June 10, 1994.

4. Nadine Joseph, Pamela G. Krupke, Bonnie Fischer, and Regina Elam, *Newsweek* Special Issue: "The New Teens," "The New Rules of Courtship," Summer/Fall 1990, 27.

5. *Youth Worker Update*, A Youth Specialties Publication, Vol. IV, No. 4, December 1989, El Cajon, CA.

6. Patricia Freeman, *People*, "Risky Business," November 5, 1990, 52.

7. John Johnson and Steve Padilla, *Los Angeles Times*, "Satanism: Growing Concern and Skepticism," Section A, April 23, 1991, 19-20.

8. Ron Harris, *Los Angeles Times*, "Children Who Dress for Excess," Section A, November 12, 1989, 1.

9. Alcohol Research Information Service, "The Bottom Line on Alcohol in Society," Vol. 8, No. 4, Winter 1988, 11.

10. Joseph Pereira, *The Wall Street Journal,* "Shunned Lessons: Even a School that Is a Leader in Drug War Grades Itself a Failure," November 10, 1989.

CHAPTER TWO

1. John and Linda Friel, *Adult Children: The Secrets of Dysfunctional Families* (Health Communications, Inc., 1988), 53.

CHAPTER FOUR

1. Jolene L. Roehlkepartain, *Parents of Teenagers,* "The Lure of MTV," December 91/January 92.
2. *Youth Worker Update,* A Youth Specialties Publication, September 1991, El Cajon, CA.
3. Jolene L. Roehlkepartain, *Parents of Teenagers,* "The Lure of MTV," December 91/January 92.
4. Al Menconi, *This Side Up,* "Rock Music, What Every Parent Should Know," 1991, Anaheim, CA.
5. Dr. Peter L. Benson, Search Institute, "The Troubled Journey: A Portrait of 6th to 12th Grade Youth," Vol. VI, No. 3, December 1990; 122 W. Franklin, Suite 525, Minneapolis, MN 55404, 612/870-9511.
6. *Chemical People* newsletter, July/August 1990.

CHAPTER FIVE

1. For more information about an experience like this with your son or daughter, call or write:

   > The National Institute of Youth Ministry
   > P. O. Box 4374
   > San Clemente, CA 92674
   > (719)498-4418

   Or, for a more extensive discussion of the issue from the teenager's point of view, read Jim Burns, *Radical Respect: A Christian Approach to Love, Sex and Dating* (Eugene, OR: Harvest House, 1991), "The Sexual Purity Challenge," chapter 4.

2. Dave Rice, Ph.D., Seminar tape for *This Side Up*, "Understanding Your Teenager in 50 Minutes or Less," National Institute of Youth Ministry, San Clemente, CA, 1994.

3. *USA Today,* January 6, 1992.

4. John Nieder, *Discipleship Journal*, Issue 64, 1991, used by permission of John Nieder, Art of Family Living, Dallas, TX.

5. Jim Burns, *Radical Respect: A Christian Approach to Love, Sex and Dating* (Eugene, OR: Harvest House, 1991), "The Sexual Purity Challenge," chapter 4.

CHAPTER SIX

1. Stephen Arterburn and Jim Burns, *Drug-Proof Your Kids* (Ventura, CA: Regal Books, 1995), 12.

2. Tom Parker, *In One Day: The Things Americans Do in One Day* (Boston: Houghton Mifflin Co., 1984), 31.

3. *Youth Worker Update*, "Parents May Be Encouraging Kids to Smoke Pot," September 1986, 3.

4. Jerry Adler, *Newsweek*, "Hour by Hour Crack," November 28, 1988, 65.

5. Tom Parker, *In One Day: The Things Americans Do In One Day* (Boston: Houghton Mifflin Co., 1984), 31.

6. New York National Council on Alcoholism, "Facts on Alcoholism and Alcohol-Related Problems," 1988, 6.

7. *The Gallup Report*, "Alcohol Use and Abuse in America," No. 265, October 1987, 44.

8. *U.S. News and World Report*, "Coming to Grips with Alcoholism," November 30, 1987, 56.

9. Alcohol Research Information Service, "The Bottom Line on Alcohol in Society," Vol. 8, No. 4, winter 1988, 11.

10. *Ibid*, 15.

11. Donald W. Goodwin, M.D., *Is Alcoholism Hereditary?* (New York: Ballantine Books, Inc., 1988), 63.

12. Arterburn and Burns, *Drug-Proof Your Kids*, 111-13.

CHAPTER EIGHT

1. Jim Burns, *Youth Builder* (Eugene, OR:

Harvest House, 1988), questionnaire used with permission.

CHAPTER NINE

1. Nina Kilham, *Seventeen*, "Satanism," August 1990, 283-85.
2. *Los Angeles Times*, Section A, April 23, 1991, 20.
3. Johanna Michaelson, *Like Lambs to a Slaughter* (Eugene, OR: Harvest House, 1980), 262.
4. Sandi Gallant as quoted by Esther Davidowitz, *Redbook*, "Die Mother, Father, Brother," April 1989, 170.

CHAPTER TEN

1. Frank Pittman, M.D., *New Woman*, "Man Enough," February 1991.

CHAPTER ELEVEN

1. *American Health*, "AIDS on Campus," March 1988, editorial.
2. Mary-Ann Shafer, M.D., with Florence Isaacs. Information is paraphrased from the article "Teenagers and AIDS" (feature of the monthly health column "The Better Way") from *Good Housekeeping*, May 1990.
3. Jerry Arterburn, *How Will I Tell My Mother?* (Nashville, TN: Oliver-Nelson, 1988), 138.

CHAPTER TWELVE

1. For information on the physiological aspects of sexual addiction, see Stephen Arterburn, *Addicted to Love* (Ann Arbor, MI: Servant Publications, 1991).

2. *Focus on the Family* Magazine, "Fatal Addiction: Ted Bundy's Final Interview with Dr. James Dobson," 1989.

3. Kenneth Kantzer, *Christianity Today*, April 17, 1987, research cited in an editorial.

4. Jim Burns, *Radical Respect: A Christian Approach to Love, Sex, and Dating* (Eugene, OR: Harvest House, 1991). This is another book by Jim Burns that is a learning experience for parents and kids (chapter 22 relates specifically to pornography). The emphasis is on discussion and interaction, goal setting, and decision making, thinking critically about important issues, and relating with peers and adults.

5. Kenneth Kantzer, *Christianity Today*, April 17, 1987, editorial.

CHAPTER THIRTEEN

1. GAO Report HRD 90-45, "Homeless and Runaway Youth Receiving Services at Federally Funded Shelters," *Homelessness*, December 1989.

2. Della Hughes, "Running Away," *USA Today*, September 1989, 64.

3. Leslie Morgan, "Desperate Odds," *Seventeen*, March 1989, 257.

4. *Ibid*, 283.

5. National Runaway Switchboard, Chicago, IL.

6. "Runaway/Homeless Youths: California's Effort to Recycle Society's Throwaways." Little Hoover Commission Report, April 1990.

CHAPTER FOURTEEN

1. D'Arcy Jennish with Sharon Doyle, "Tragic Obsession," *Macleans*, October 9, 1989.

2. *Ibid*.

3. *Ibid*.

4. Statistics from a report in the *New England Journal of Medicine*, August 1985.

5. American Psychiatric Association, *The Diagnostic and Statistical Manual of Mental Disorders, Fourth Edition* (Washington, D.C.: APA, 1980).

6. Joan Jacobs Bramberg, *Fasting Girls: The Emergence of Anorexia Nervosa as a Modern Disease,* as quoted in *Harper's* Magazine, "Social History," August 1989, 31.

7. *Ibid*, 32.

8. Karen Lehman, *Anorexia and Bulimia: Causes and Cures*, Consumers Research, September 1981, 29.

9. American Psychiatric Association, *The Diagnostic and Statistical Manual of Mental Disorders, Fourth Edition* (Washington, D.C.: APA, 1980).

CHAPTER FIFTEEN

1. Gary Smalley, *The Keys to Your Child's Heart* (Dallas, TX: Word, Inc., 1992), 82.

2. Ross Campbell, *How to Really Love Your Child* (Wheaton, IL: Victor Books, 1977), 42.

CHAPTER SIXTEEN

1. For a sheet discussing some possible resources and family devotional learning experiences, call or write:

   > The National Institute of Youth Ministry
   > P. O. Box 4374
   > San Clemente, CA 92674
   > 714 498-4418

2. James Dobson, *Dr. Dobson Answers Your Questions* (Wheaton, IL: Tyndale House, 1982).

Referrals

CHAPTER THREE

Transitional Generation
Focus on the Family—719/531-3400 ext. 2300
    (Can provide Christian counseling referrals.)
    Colorado Springs, CO 80995

CHAPTER FIVE

Sex
Josh McDowell Ministries—800/222-JOSH
    P.O. Box 1000
    Dallas, TX 75221

National Institute of Youth Ministry—
    800/397-9725
    P.O. Box 4374
    San Clemente, CA 92674

CHAPTER SIX

Substance Abuse
New Life Clinics—
    800/639-5433 (NEW-LIFE)
    3933 S. Broadway
    St. Louis, MO 63118

Teen Challenge—417/862-6969
    P.O. Box 1015
    Springfield, MO 65801

CHAPTER SEVEN

Sexual Abuse

New Life Clinics—
   800/639-5433 (NEW-LIFE)
   3933 S. Broadway,
   St. Louis, MO 63118

CHAPTER EIGHT

Suicide

National Runaway Switchboard and Suicide
   Hotline 800/621-4000 or 312/880-9860

CHAPTER NINE

Satanism

Exodus—512/490-3857
   P.O. Box 700293
   San Antonio, TX 78720

C.O.I.N. (Christian Occult & Investigative
   Network)
   1432 W. Puente Ave.
   West Covina, CA 91790

CHAPTER TEN

Homosexuality

Exodus International—415/454-1017
   P.O. Box 2121
   San Rafael, CA 94912

Desert Stream—714/779-6899
   P.O. Box 17635
   Anaheim, CA 92817

Spatula Ministries
P.O. Box 444
La Habra, CA 90631
(Restore families with homosexual members)

Love in Action—901/542-0250
P.O. Box 753307
Memphis, TN 38175-3307

CHAPTER ELEVEN
AIDS
Desert Stream—714/779-6899
P.O. Box 17635
Anaheim, CA 92817

New Life Clinics—
800/639-5433 (NEW LIFE)
3933 S. Broadway
St. Louis, MO 63118

CHAPTER TWELVE
Pornography
National Coalition Against Pornography—
513/521-6227
800 Compton Rd., Ste. 9224
Cincinnati, OH 45231

Pure Life Ministries—606/824-4444
P.O. Box 410
Dry Ridge, KY 41035

CHAPTER THIRTEEN

Runaways

Runaway Hotline, Austin, TX—800/231-6946

Hit Home—800/448-4663

Covenant House 9 Line—800/999-9999,
213/613-0300 (fax)
460 W. 41st Street
New York, NY 10036

National Runaway Switchboard—800/621-4000

Missing Children HELP Center—800/872-5437
410 Ware Blvd., Ste. 400
Tampa, FL 33619

CHAPTER FOURTEEN

Eating Disorders
New Life Clinics—
800/639-5433 (NEW-LIFE)
3933 S. Broadway
St. Louis, MO 63118

Remuda Ranch—800/445-1900
Jack Burden Rd., Box 2481
Wickenburg, AZ 85358

Focus on the Family does not endorse these referrals in their entirety.

Books and References

These books and resources are available from

National Institute of Youth Ministry
P. O. Box 4374
San Clemente, CA 92674.
(714) 498-4418
(800) 397-9725

Books for Parents:

Drug-Proof Your Kids
   Solid biblical principles combined with effective prevention and intervention techniques for parents of teens.

Dear Dad . . . If I Could Tell You Anything
   Touching and inspirational messages that will draw you closer to your child by discovering what he or she thinks, feels, and needs.

Books for Students:
(Each book includes discussion starters, action steps, family and group experiences, and Bible study.)

Radical Love
   A book that gets down to core issues that are vital to healthy, joy-filled relationships for students in today's world.

Getting in Touch with God
An inspiring devotional for spiritual growth.

90 Days through the New Testament
A three-month program of spiritual growth and discipline.

Spirit Wings
A spirit-filled devotional to "take off" in your relationship with God.

For Youth Workers:

The Youth Builder
Proven methods, specific recommendations, and hands-on examples of handling and understanding the challenges of youth ministry.

High School Ministry
Learn about the influence of high school culture and discover the impact you can have on your students.

The Youth Workers Book of Case Studies
Fifty-two stories with discussion questions to add interest to Bible studies.

Curriculum for Youth Workers and Christian Schools:

The Word on Sex, Drugs, and Rock 'n' Roll
Gives youth a biblical framework for making good choices in life.

The Word on Prayer and the Devotional Life

Help youth get closer to God by getting a grip on prayer.

The Word on the Basics of Christianity

Here are the foundational truths of Christianity, presented in an active format.

The Word on Being a Leader, Serving Others and Sharing Your Faith

Students can serve God and each other by taking an active role in leadership.

The Word on Helping a Friend in Crisis

Young people can discover what God's Word says about crisis issues and how to help others.

The Word on the Life and Ministry of Christ

Discover more about Jesus Christ through this story of His life on earth.

The Word on Finding and Using Your Spiritual Gifts

You'll discover your God-given special gift and find ways to use it in your spiritual life.

Focus on the Family does not endorse these resources in their entirety. We suggest you evaluate them personally.

Other Books to Strengthen Your Relationships
From Focus on the Family®

Give Them Wings
When kids hit their teenage years, the role of parents begins to change. In *Give Them Wings*, author Carol Kuykendall offers encouragement for raising kids to be responsible, godly men and women and for looking toward the empty nest with hope. Paperback.

Once a Parent, Always a Parent
Kids grow up, but they're still your kids! Steven Bly in *Once a Parent, Always a Parent*, shares practical ways to become involved—but not over-involved— in your adult child's life. Learn how to best provide support, encouragement, financial assistance, childcare and much more whether your child lives across the country or across the hall. Paperback.

Guiding Your Family in a Misguided World
With all the mixed messages society spouts, Tony Evans' *Guiding Your Family in a Misguided World* is an indispensable guide for creating a stable, Christ-centered home, developing a strong personal faith and living a life that's pleasing to God. Paperback.

Look for these special books in your Christian bookstore or request a copy by calling 1-800-A-FAMILY (1-800-232-6459). Friends in Canada may write Focus on the Family, P.O. Box 9800, Stn. Terminal, Vancouver, B.C. V6B 4G3 or call 1-800-661-9800.

Visit our Web site (www.family.org) to learn more about the ministry or to find out if there is a Focus on the Family office in your country.

FOCUS ON THE FAMILY®
Welcome to the Family!

Whether you received this book as a gift, borrowed it from
a friend, or purchased it yourself, we're glad you read it!
It's just one of the many helpful, insightful and encouraging
resources produced by Focus on the Family.

In fact, that's what Focus on the Family is all about—
providing inspiration, information and biblically based
advice to people in all stages of life.

It began in 1977 with the vision of one man, Dr. James Dobson,
a licensed psychologist and author of 16 best-selling books on
marriage, parenting, and family. Alarmed by the societal, political,
and economic pressures that were threatening the existence
of the American family, Dr. Dobson founded Focus on the Family
with one employee—an assistant—and a once-a-week
radio broadcast, aired on only 36 stations.

Now an international organization, Focus on the Family is
dedicated to preserving Judeo-Christian values and strengthening
the family through more than 70 different ministries, including
eight separate daily radio broadcasts; television public service
announcements; 11 publications; and a steady series of books
and award-winning films and videos for people
of all ages and interests.

Recognizing the needs of, as well as the sacrifices and important
contribution made by, such diverse groups as educators, physi-
cians, attorneys, crisis pregnancy center staff and single parents,
Focus on the Family offers specific outreaches to uphold and minister to these individuals, too. And it's all done for one purpose,
and one purpose only: to encourage and strengthen individuals
and families through the life-changing message of Jesus Christ.

• • •

For more information about the ministry, or if we can be of help to
your family, simply write to Focus on the Family, Colorado Springs,
CO 80995 or call 1-800-A-FAMILY (1-800-232-6459). Friends in
Canada may write Focus on the Family, P.O. Box 9800, Stn.
Terminal, Vancouver, B.C. V6B 4G3 or call 1-800-661-9800. Visit our
Web site—www.family.org—to learn more about the ministry or to
find out if there is a Focus on the Family office in your country.

We'd love to hear from you!